Alan Robinson qualified as a solicitor in 1972 and has spent the whole of his working life involved with two areas of law – welfare law and work with charities and voluntary organisations. He retired from legal practice in 2010, having been running his own firm for a number of years, and now works part-time as a consultant and trainer. Alan has worked in and taught community care law from its inception in 1993.

Introduction to the Law of Community Care in England and Wales

Introduction to the Law of Community Care in England and Wales

Alan Robinson,

MA (York), MA (Sheffield),

LL.B (London), Solicitor

Law Brief Publishing

Published 2017 by
Law Brief Publishing
30 The Parks
Minehead
Somerset
TA24 8BT

www.lawbriefpublishing.com

Paperback: 978-1-911035-38-1

PREFACE

The aim of this work is to introduce the system of community care as it operates in both England and Wales. Prior to 2014, the law in both countries was governed by the NHS & Community Care Act 1990, and the legislation for which that Act provided a framework. Following the work of the Law Commission in developing the new law, the Care Act 2014 came into force in England on 1st April 2015, while the previous law continued to operate in Wales. On 6th April 2016, the Social Services and Well Being (Wales) Act 2014 came into force in Wales. There are many significant differences between the two codes, not least in that the Welsh approach is to incorporate services for children, whereas the English law is in large measure concerned with the law as it affects adults.

However, community care is not just about the Care Act 2014 or about the Social Services and Well-Being (Wales) Act 2014. Since the Welsh Assembly has chosen to develop its own approach, the effect now is that there are different statutory approaches in the two countries, although both are underpinned by law which is frequently common to both jurisdictions, consisting of both common law and statutes such as the Mental Capacity Act 2005. The book therefore proceeds by firstly setting out separate sections on the statutory law and guidance in England and the statutory law and guidance in Wales, and secondly by including a section which covers the common provisions.

The point should also be made that certain common provisions appear in the Care Act 2014, and Welsh readers may need to have recourse to that Act for some matters of detail.

The reader, depending on whether he or she is practising in England or in Wales, should therefore be able to read the relevant section on the community care law properly so called, and also to read the relevant parts of part D of this work to expand on the information so obtained.

Any errors are the author's. The law is stated as at 31st July 2017.

Alan Robinson
July 2017

Contents

PART A –
THE LAW BEFORE 2014

Before the new legislation was introduced, there were two strands to community care law which had attracted criticism over time; the kind of services available, including the method of gaining access to them and the rationing caused by funding limitations; and the process of paying for them. The Law Commission was asked to consider the legislation as a whole, and produced and consulted on proposals for change. The Law Commission recommended replacing the complex provisions then in place, governed by the **NHS & Community Care Act 1990,** with a single statute, together with detail in regulations, and a Code of Practice. The Government then published its proposals in a White Paper ("*Caring for our Future: Reforming Care and Support*") with a draft Care Bill attached.

The **NHS & Community Care Act 1990** had operated by imposing a framework over a series of existing local authority powers and duties. There were five defined "community care services" which were:-

- The provision of accommodation under sec 21 **National Assistance Act 1948**;
- The provision of services for people who are disabled, under sec 29 **National Assistance Act 1948**;
- The provision of after-care services under sec 117 **Mental Health Act 1983**, for those who had been detained for treatment under that Act;
- The provision of services for "older people" contained in a power found in the **Health Services and Public Health Act 1968**; and
- The provision of home helps, and laundry facilities, under the **Health Act 2006.**

Section 47 of the 1990 Act required local authorities to respond to an appearance of need for any of these services by carrying out an assessment. Subject to the individual qualifying for services by meeting the eligibility criteria, there might be a duty or a power to provide services. There was not a general duty to meet a need whatever it was, so someone whose needs did not fall straightforwardly within one of the powers and duties listed above (for instance, someone with an addiction to drugs or alcohol) would not necessarily qualify for services. The other restriction inherent in the scheme as it had evolved was the right which local authorities had to allocate resources according to their own financial situation; this was confirmed initially by the decision of the House of Lords in **R v Gloucestershire County Council ex parte Barry** [1997] **2 WLR 459**, which held that, although an authority could not restrict need by pleading their own financial constraints in a specific case, they would be expected to set down eligibility criteria in categories, and to decide (in practice by reference to their finances) to which categories of need they would allocate services. In due course national guidance was issued setting out four potential categories of need; critical, substantial, moderate and low.

The consequence for the individual was that his or her access to services was determined according to which category he or she fell into. Overall, the effect was not a system which would meet needs, but rather a system which had various services available to those who qualified for them.

It should also be noted that, apart from the statutes listed above, there were a number of other statutes which were relevant, of which probably the **Chronically Sick and Disabled Persons Act 1970**, setting out services for disabled people, was the most significant. In addition, law could be found in regulations, and in directions issued by the Secretary of State under section 7 of the **Local Authority Social Services Act 1970**; and in various levels of guidance, issued both nationally and locally.

This situation was then superseded by the introduction of two statutes. In England, the **Care Act 2014** came into force on 1st April 2015; and in Wales, the **Social Services and Well-Being (Wales) Act 2014** came into force on 6th April 2016. The two Acts do not cover precisely the same ground; indeed, the effect is the creation of two separate and distinct care regimes. The Welsh Act also covers the provision of services to young people with needs, and to young carers, which therefore provides a seamless transition from childhood to adulthood. In England, coverage of children will largely remain the province of the **Children Act 1989** as amended by the **Children and Families Act 2014**.

PART B –
THE LAW IN ENGLAND

CHAPTER ONE: THE STRUCTURE OF THE CARE ACT 2014

1. General principles

The Act set out to regularise the confusing collection of statutes which governed community care in England, which are described above in Part A. The **Care Act 2014** regulates the provision of services in England (but not in Wales) from April 2015.

The Act also covers changes to the system of paying for care. Certain other changes to the system of payment were due to be implemented in April 2016, but this has now been postponed until April 2020, and this is described below. Meanwhile the system which now regulates payment, which still in large measure reflects the system in place before April 2015, as amended by the Act, is described in Chapter 4.

With limited exceptions, the Act repeals almost all of the principal adult care statutes, including the **National Assistance Act 1948** and the **NHS & Community Care Act 1990**. Some 20 sets of new regulations were also issued. The Law Commission had recommended a Code of Practice, but instead there is statutory guidance. The guidance extends to some 500 pages.

The Statutory Guidance has already been updated on several occasions, most recently on 28 June 2017. It is now only available online, and can be consulted at https://www.gov.uk/guidance/care-and-support-statutory-guidance. The amendments have been necessary to take account of some of the issues that have arisen since the Act became law, especially the rules on ordinary residence as they are interpreted following the decision of the Supreme Court in **R (Cornwall) v Secretary of State for Health [2015] UKSC 46.** Ordinary residence is considered in Chapter 6 of Part D.

The full regime under the Act has not yet been implemented. The Government had indicated its intention of creating an appeals process, and consulted on a proposal to do so by regulation under section 72 of the Act. The consultation was completed on 30 March 2015, but is apparently still under consideration within Government. The other significant item which remains in limbo, as noted above, is the further amendment to the system of paying for care, in particular the care cap, for which see further below, especially in Chapter 3 of this Part.

One of the problems which has been identified with the **Care Act 2014** is that it is concerned with 'adults', but that some of the legislation which it replaced, such as the **Chronically Sick and Disabled Persons Act 1970,** also covers people under 18, so that the repeal of that statute can only be partial. Many of the problems which had been identified as concerning the rights of children, young carers, and disabled children with parent carers have now been addressed, some in the **Care Act 2014** and others in the **Children and Families Act 2014**. These measures are considered separately.

The Act is concerned with 'adults' and 'carers'. As noted in Chapter 2, the previous definition of a carer was replaced by a new definition in the **Care Act 2014**.

2. The general duties of the local authority

The Act contains a series of general duties. The first, in section 1, is a duty to promote the 'well-being' of individuals, i.e. adults and carers. Well-being includes:

- personal dignity, physical and mental health, and emotional well-being;
- protection from abuse and neglect;
- control over day-to-day life;
- participation in work, education, training or recreation;

- social and economic well-being;
- domestic, family and personal relationships;
- suitability of living accommodation; and
- the individual's contribution to society.

The term 'choice' does not appear.

In fulfilling this duty, the local authority is required to have regard to:

- The assumption that an individual is best placed to judge his or her well-being;
- The individual's views, wishes, feelings and beliefs;
- The taking into account of all the individual's circumstances, and the need to make decisions that are not based on stereotyping individuals;
- The importance of individuals participating as fully as possible in relevant decisions (including provision to them of necessary information and support);
- The importance of achieving a 'balance between the individual's wellbeing and that of any friends or relatives who are involved in caring for the individual';
- The need to protect people from abuse and neglect;
- The need to ensure that restrictions on individual rights/freedoms be kept to the minimum necessary.

There are echoes here of the **Mental Capacity Act 2005**, although it was expressly decided that the **Care Act 2014** should not contain a set of principles.

There is no specific reference to independent living, which is protected by **Article 19** of the **UN Convention on the Rights of Persons with Disabilities**. However, the statutory guidance states:-

> "*The wellbeing principle is intended to cover the key components of independent living, as expressed in the [Convention], (in particular Article 19 of the Convention). Supporting people to live as independently as possible, for as long as possible, is a guiding principle of the Care Act.*" (para 1.19).

Given the willingness of the courts to have regard to the European Convention (see for example **Burnip v Birmingham City Council [2012] EWCA Civ 629,** and **R (Bracking) v SSWP [2013] EWCA Civ 1345),** there may be a tendency to seek to use the Convention to secure rights under the Act. See also for example **Mathieson v Secretary of State for Work and Pensions [2015] UKSC 47.**

There is now authority on the application of the well-being principle, which is discussed in Part D below, in particular the cases of **R (Davey) v Oxfordshire County Council [2017] EWHC 354,** and **R (JF) v Merton LBC [2017] EWHC 1519 (Admin).**

Under section 2, local authorities are under a general duty to provide a range of preventative services in order to prevent or delay the development of needs for care and support by individuals including carers, and to reduce those needs where they exist. This is unlikely to lead, at a time of financial strain on local authorities, to significant improvements in the preventative services available; but it may prove a more valuable provision in the future.

There is a duty under section 3 to promote integration with health provision where it would promote well-being and/or contribute to the prevention of the development of needs, and/or improve the quality of care.

Local authorities have an enhanced duty to ensure that adults in need and carers are provided with information about care and support arrangements under section 4. The requirement is not that the authority itself must make provision, but that it must ensure that suitable provision is in place. Face to face contact is considered preferable, and an online service alone is unlikely to meet the expectations.

One of the problems of the former system is the lack of availability of high quality providers, coupled with issues of the instability of some large providers, as exemplified by the collapse in 2011 of the independent company known as Southern Cross, which was at the time providing 752 care homes. There is therefore a range of provision in the Act, and in three sets of regulations, designed to address those problems by increasing diversity. This is to be found in section 5 of the Act, as well as in the **Care and Support (Market Oversight Information) Regulations 2014 SI 2014/2822**, and the **Care and Support (Market Oversight Criteria) Regulations 2015 SI 2015/314.** There is also provision for dealing with cross-border issues in the **Care and Support (Cross-Border Placements and Business Failure: Temporary Duty) (Dispute Resolution) Regulations 2014 SI 2014/2843.**

There are further duties to co-operate; section 6 creates a general duty on a local authority to co-operate with its "relevant partners" and section 7 creates a specific duty for a relevant partner to do so when requested by a local authority. "Relevant partners" include other local authorities, NHS bodies, the Crown, the police and probation services.

CHAPTER TWO: ASSESSMENT IN ENGLAND

1. The Single Assessment

An **assessment** is the process of considering a person's circumstances and making a decision about whether they need care and support to help them live their day-to-day lives. The assessment for care and support is usually carried out by a social worker, and will consider the presenting needs as well as the person's other circumstances.

Under the former system, following the determination of needs, the local authority was required to consider what eligible services to provide. They did so using an eligibility framework, which was laid down in guidance. Which needs were eligible for services was a matter for the authority under the guidance; but once the service user was assessed as eligible, the authority had a duty to provide the service (see Lord Wilson in **R (KM) v Cambridgeshire County Council, [2012] UKSC 23**). The consequence of non-standard eligibility criteria was that what constituted eligible needs varied from one area to another. It is also important to note that local authorities were able to determine to which categories of people they planned to provide support by reference to their own financial situation, i.e. they might have provided services to those in all four categories of need (critical, substantial, moderate and low), or to only three, or two, or even one. Most authorities were providing services to those in the critical and substantial categories. See **R v Gloucestershire County Council ex parte Barry** [1997] **2 WLR 459.**

The **Care Act 2014** creates (in section 9) a single duty for local authorities to carry out assessments in order to determine whether an adult has needs for care and support. The assessment:

- must be of the adult's needs and the outcomes they want to achieve;
- must be provided to all people who appear to have some need for care and support, and therefore should not consider unrelated factors such as a person's finances;

- must not consider whether the local authority thinks the person will be eligible for services (see **R v Bristol CC ex parte Penfold (1998) 1 CCLR 315**); and
- must be carried out with involvement from the adult and, where appropriate, their carer or someone else they nominate.

Unlike the previous legislation, there is no categorisation of individuals according to type (so for example the definition of a disabled person, formerly in the **National Assistance Act 1948**, disappears). Nor is there a list of potential services. There is an illustrative list in section 8(1) of what **may** be provided to an adult or carer, including

- accommodation in a care home or other premises;
- care and support at home or in the community;
- counselling, advocacy and other types of social work;
- goods and facilities;
- information and advice.

Items such as 'adaptations', 'travel' and 'holidays', which were included in the **Chronically Sick and Disabled Persons Act 1970** sec 2, do not appear in the new legislation. In response to an enquiry from the Select Committee, the Department of Health confirmed that they considered that those services did fall within the new system. The Guidance says,

> *"The concept of 'meeting needs' is intended to be broader than a duty to provide or arrange a particular service. Because a person's needs are specific to them, there are many ways in which their needs can be met. The intention behind the legislation is to encourage this diversity, rather than point to a service or solution that may be neither what is best nor what the person wants." (10.10)*

Local authorities can delegate all their functions under the Act, with the exception of the safeguarding provisions (under secs 42-47) and charging. This includes assessment. Under the old law, authorities could delegate assessment, provide that they signed off the recommendations; the signing off itself can now be delegated. No charge can be made for assessment; as the Minister (Norman Lamb MP) said, the provisions do "not give a power to local authorities to charge for carrying out a needs or carer's assessment in any circumstances."

The **Care and Support (Eligibility Criteria) Regulations 2015 SI 2015/313** (the Eligibility Regulations) make clear that the determination of an adult's eligible needs is made without taking into account any support which is already being provided by a carer. "Instead, where a person receives support from a carer, this will be taken into account during the development of the care and support plan", according to a discussion document in 2013. The term used for this is "carer blind assessments". In other words, a person may not be denied care and support because it is already being provided by a carer. The position is different in Wales (see below).

After conducting the needs assessment, the local authority is then required to determine whether the person has eligible needs, using an eligibility framework which is now statutory and no longer contained in guidance. The previous categories of need ('critical', 'substantial', 'moderate', and 'low') have disappeared, and there is now a national standard for eligibility.

2. Entitlement to Care and Support

The intention was to address the previous situation of different statutes and different levels of entitlement for care and support. For example, the legal test for the provision of residential accommodation was significantly different from the test for the provision of domiciliary care. The intention was also to remove some of the anomalies in the legislation which create different entitlements for different groups of people.

The Act sets out to create a single, consistent route to establishing an entitlement to care and support for all adults. It also creates an entitlement to support for carers, on a similar basis.

Under Regulation 2 of the Eligibility Regulations, an adult must satisfy three requirements:-

- their needs must result from a physical or mental impairment or illness;
- as a result they must be unable to achieve **two or more** specified outcomes; and
- as a consequence, there must be (or be likely to be) a **significant** impact on their well-being.

A person is 'unable' to achieve an outcome if they:-

- are unable to achieve it without assistance;
- are able to achieve it without assistance but only where it causes them significant pain, distress or anxiety;
- or able to achieve it without assistance but doing so will endanger their health or safety, or that of others, or
- achieving it would take significantly longer than would normally be expected.

The outcomes are:-

- managing and maintaining nutrition;
- managing personal hygiene;
- managing toilet needs;
- being appropriately clothed;

- being able to make use of their home safely;
- maintaining a habitable home environment;
- developing and maintaining family or other personal relationships;
- accessing and engaging in work, training, education or volunteering;
- making use of necessary facilities or services in the local community including public transport; and
- carrying out caring responsibilities which the person has for a child.

The term "physical or mental impairment" is not defined by the Act, but paragraph 6.104 of the Guidance says that this refers to "physical, mental, sensory, learning or cognitive disabilities or illnesses, substance misuse or brain injury." It is clear that this wide interpretation is intended to encompass such descriptions as "any disorder or disability of the mind" as in section 1 of the **Mental Health Act 1983.**

The guidance states (para 6.115):-

> "*The eligibility determination must be made based on the adult's needs and how these impact on their wellbeing. Authorities must only take consideration of whether the adult has a carer, or what needs may be met by a carer after the eligibility determination when a care and support plan is prepared. The determination must be based solely on the adult's needs and if an adult does have a carer, the care they are providing will be taken into account when considering whether the needs must be met.*"

The eligibility criteria may be overridden in case of emergency, as with the old law.

3. Refusal of an assessment

Under section 11, a person may refuse an assessment; if they do so, the duty of the local authority is generally discharged. However, there are two exceptions: the first is where the person lacks capacity and an assessment is in their best interests, and the second is where the person is at risk of abuse or neglect.

4. The Law for Carers

Carers had the right to an assessment under the old law, but they had no right to any services at all, and any services were provided on a purely discretionary basis. The Act gives a right to services for all adult carers. There are also provisions to assist carers under the age of 18 in the transition from being a young carer (and therefore covered by the **Children Act 1989**) to becoming an adult carer (and therefore covered by the **Care Act 2014**).

A carer is an adult who is helping another person, usually a relative or friend, in the activities of their day-to-day life. This is not the same as someone who provides care professionally, or gives their time to care through a voluntary organisation – these categories of carer are specifically excluded. The Act provides (in section 10(3)) that a carer is anyone who provides, or intends to provide, care and support.

Under the **Carers (Recognition and Services) Act 1995**, section 1(1)(b), caring arises where:

> *"an individual ("the carer") provides or intends to provide a substantial amount of care on a regular basis for the relevant person."*

This limitation has been removed by the **Care Act**. Section 10 (3) defines a carer thus:

> *"Carer" means an adult who provides or intends to provide care for another adult*

The requirement that care be "regular and substantial" has been removed.

"Care" is not defined. The guidance states at para 6.18 that the term covers both practical and emotional support.

Legislation for carers was previously to be found in three different statutes, the **Carers (Recognition and Services) Act 1995, the Carers and Disabled Children Act 2000,** and the **Carers (Equal Opportunities) Act 2004.** The provisions of all three Acts have been superseded by the new legislation.

4.1 Carers' Assessments

The Act creates a single duty (in Section 10) for local authorities to undertake a 'carer's assessment'. This replaces the existing law, and removes the requirement that the carer must be providing "a substantial amount of care on a regular basis". This will mean more carers are able to access an assessment, and that the duty is comparable to that which is owed to the people they support.

The aim of the assessment is to consider the impact of caring on the carer and to ascertain

- whether the carer is willing and able to carry on caring;
- the impact on the carer's wellbeing;
- the outcomes which the carer wishes in day-to-day life;
- whether the carer works, or wishes to work, or to participate in education, training and recreation.

If both the carer and the person they care for agree, a joint assessment of both their needs can be undertaken. A combined assessment cannot be imposed.

The assessment should seek to establish not just the carer's needs for support but also the sustainability of the carer's role.

The carer may refuse the assessment; in this case the local authority's duty is discharged, but the carer can ask again for an assessment.

An assessment should be proportionate ("light touch" where appropriate). There is provision for advocates where necessary.

4.2 Eligibility

When the assessment is complete, the local authority must determine what their needs for support are, and whether those needs are 'eligible' for support.

The local authority must use the eligibility framework which is set out in regulations. **Regulation 3** of the **Care and Support (Eligibility Criteria) Regulations 2015 SI 2015/313** provides that a carer's needs meet the eligibility criteria if:-

- the needs arise as a consequence of providing necessary care for an adult;
- the effect of the carer's needs is that any of the circumstances set out below apply to the carer;
- as a consequence there is, or is likely to be, a significant impact on the carer's wellbeing.

The circumstances are:-

(a) the carer's physical or mental health is, or is at risk of, deteriorating; or

(b) the carer is unable to achieve any of the following outcomes:

- carrying out any caring responsibilities the carer has for a child;
- providing care to other persons for whom the carer provides care;
- maintaining a habitable home environment in the carers home (whether or not this is also the home of the adult needing care);
- managing and maintaining nutrition;
- developing and maintaining family or other personal relationships;
- engaging in work, training, education or volunteering;
- making use of necessary facilities or services in the local community, including recreational facilities or services; and
- engaging in recreational activities.

The question is whether the carer needs support. The question whether the person being cared for is in need of care and support under the Act is irrelevant to the carer's assessment.

Section 20 imposes a duty on the local authority, equivalent to that owed to a person in need of care and support, to meet a carer's need for support if the criteria are met. This is one of the most significant changes in the Act; previously carers were entitled to an assessment but had no entitlement to services.

5. Young people including young carers

Sections 58-59 of the Act require a local authority to undertake a needs assessment of a disabled child if it considers that the child is likely to have needs for care and support after becoming 18, and the assessment is likely to be of 'significant benefit" to the child. The guidance says that this refers to the likely needs of the child, in the same way as for an adult, and (presumably) this means that a child will not have to meet the definition of disabled child in section 17(10) of the **Children Act 1989**, which is itself based on the outdated (and now repealed) definition in section 29 of the **National Assistance Act 1948**. It is not clear why the "significant benefit" qualification was added. Once the child reaches 18, he or she will in any event be entitled to an assessment under the provisions outlined above.

Sections 60 to 62 place a similar duty on the local authority to assess the disabled child's adult carers if the carer is likely to have needs for support once the child reaches 18.

Children under the age of 18 who care for adults (young carers) will be provided with children's services (probably as children in need, under section 17 **Children Act 1989**), rather than adult care and support. However, when they reach the age of 18, the responsibility for their support will switch to adult services. Under sections 63 and 64, adult services will take part in transition planning before the carer is 18, and will have a duty to continue to provide services after 18 if adult carer services are not yet in place.

CHAPTER THREE: PROVISION OF SERVICES IN ENGLAND

1. Duty to meet care and support needs

One of the main departures within the **Care Act 2014** is that there is now a duty to provide care and support. This is covered by sections 18-20 of the Act. Where an individual's needs meet the criteria, there is a duty to ensure that their care and support needs are met, provided they are ordinarily resident in the local authority's area. Ordinary residence in discussed in Part D. If their capital or income exceeds the limits, there will nevertheless be a duty on the authority to meet the assessed needs for care and support. There is a similar duty to a carer whose needs for support meet the eligibility criteria. Where there is no duty to meet needs, section 19 nevertheless provides a power to do so.

2. Support planning

Under sections 25-26, the authority will be expected to carry out support planning with the person being cared for and/or the carer. Both are entitled under section 26 to receive a personal budget, to show them the costs of meeting their needs, and to indicate how much money is available to them. They will then (subject to having capacity) have a right to request that the local authority make a direct payment to them under section 31, to give them control over how their support is provided. All of these provisions apply equally to carers as to the people they care for. They must also have regular reviews to ensure their needs continue to be met. The result is that the pre-Care Act 2014 (guidance-based) practice of personalisation and personal budgets continues, but as a matter of law rather than of guidance.

3. Care and Support Plans

Having established whether the local authority has a duty to meet care and support needs, or is choosing to meet needs under a power, the

Act sets out what must happen next to help the adult make decisions about how their needs should be met.

There is a duty on the local authority to provide a care and support plan (or a support plan in the case of a carer) (section 25). In providing this plan, they must then work with the adult, or the carer, to help them to decide how to meet their needs, and to produce a plan which sets out the detail of what was agreed. As part of this planning process, the local authority must tell people about their right to ask for a direct payment for some or all of their needs.

One of the core requirements of a care and support plan is a personal budget for the adult and, for the first time, the Act creates a legal entitlement to a personal budget. This is intended to help people to understand the costs of meeting their needs and find out what public funding is available to help them. This is complemented by the right to request a direct payment to meet some or all of those needs, to maximise the control people have over how that money is spent.

Even in the instances when assessments have determined that adults do not have eligible needs, the local authority can advise people about what needs they do have, and how to meet them or prevent further needs from developing. The Act requires local authorities to give information to people to help them support themselves better in these circumstances (section 4).

Completing the planning process and putting in place care and support arrangements does not mean the end of the local authority's responsibilities. The local authority has a duty under section 27 to review the plan to ensure that the adult's needs and outcomes continue to be met over time.

Matters concerning personalisation and personal budgets are dealt with in Chapter 4 of this Part.

4. How is the need to be met?

The law on this topic is largely common to both England and Wales, and is therefore discussed in Part D of this work.

5. People from abroad

The law on this topic is also to be found in Part D of this work.

6. Safeguarding

Safeguarding is the term which, when used in respect of adults, describes the function of protecting them from abuse or neglect. Adults in need of care and support may be at risk of abuse or neglect, due to the actions or lack of actions of other people. There has never been a proper legal framework for this, and the **Care Act 2014** provides one (within limits), in sections 42-47.

Section 42 reads:-

> *This section has no associated Explanatory Notes*
>
> *(1) This section applies where a local authority has reasonable cause to suspect that an adult in its area (whether or not ordinarily resident there)—*
> *(a) has needs for care and support (whether or not the authority is meeting any of those needs),*
> *(b) is experiencing, or is at risk of, abuse or neglect, and*
> *(c) as a result of those needs is unable to protect himself or herself against the abuse or neglect or the risk of it.*
> *(2) The local authority must make (or cause to be made) whatever enquiries it thinks necessary to enable it to decide whether any action should be taken in the adult's case (whether under this Part or otherwise) and, if so, what and by whom.*

(3) "Abuse" includes financial abuse; and for that purpose "financial abuse" includes—
(a) having money or other property stolen,
(b) being defrauded,
(c) being put under pressure in relation to money or other property, and
(d) having money or other property misused.

The authority's duty is to enquire, and the law does not tell it what the result of its enquiry should, or could, be (c.f. section 47 **Children Act 1989**). Nor does the law provide any additional powers for the authority to deal with the results of its enquiry. Compare the Welsh Act, which gives a power of entry in order to speak to a person at risk; and the Scottish legislation, which gives a power of removal. The previous power to seek a court order for removal under section 47 of the **National Assistance Act 1948** was repealed by the **Care Act 2014**.

Although the Act gives examples of abuse, it does not explain what the term 'abuse' means. The guidance gives a much more comprehensive indication of what is meant, including:–

· *Physical abuse;*

· *Domestic violence, including psychological and emotional abuse;*

· *Sexual abuse including 'inappropriate looking or touching';*

· *Psychological abuse including 'deprivation of contact, blaming, controlling, cyber bullying, isolation';*

· *Financial or material abuse;*

· *Modern slavery;*

· *Discriminatory abuse – including forms of 'harassment, slurs or similar treatment; because of race, gender and gender identity, age, disability, sexual orientation or religion';*

· *Organisational abuse – including 'neglect and poor care practice within an institution or specific care setting such as a hospital or care home' ranging from 'one off incidents to on-going ill-treatment' and 'neglect or poor professional practice as a result of the structure, policies, processes and practices within an organisation'.*

· *Neglect and acts of omission – including 'ignoring medical, emotional or physical care needs, failure to provide access to appropriate health, care and support or educational services, the withholding of the necessities of life, such as medication, adequate nutrition and heating'*

· *Self-neglect including 'a wide range of behaviour neglecting to care for one's personal hygiene, health or surroundings and includes behaviour such as hoarding.*

Although there are no specific additional powers, there are various additional provisions. Section 43 requires the local authority to establish a Safeguarding Board for its area. The Safeguarding Adults Board (SAB) has various powers and duties, including the duty (under section 44) to establish a review in defined circumstances. Section 44 provides:-

(1) An SAB ***must*** (emphasis added) *arrange for there to be a review of a case involving an adult in its area with needs for care and support (whether or not the local authority has been meeting any of those needs) if—*
(a) there is reasonable cause for concern about how the SAB, members of it or other persons with relevant functions worked together to safeguard the adult, and
(b) condition 1 or 2 is met.

(2) Condition 1 is met if—
(a) the adult has died, and
(b) the SAB knows or suspects that the death resulted from abuse or neglect (whether or not it knew about or suspected the abuse or neglect before the adult died).

(3) Condition 2 is met if—
(a) the adult is still alive, and
(b) the SAB knows or suspects that the adult has experienced serious abuse or neglect.

> *(4) An SAB* **may** (emphasis added) *arrange for there to be a review of any other case involving an adult in its area with needs for care and support (whether or not the local authority has been meeting any of those needs).*

Given the range of duties and powers previously available (for example, the vetting and barring legislation, the **Mental Capacity Act 2005**, the **Mental Health Act 1983**, the 'No Secrets' Guidance, the inspections regime of the CQC, the **Human Rights Act** duties placed on public bodies, the criminal law, whistle-blowing, the **Health Acts**, and so on), which the Act does nothing to address, apart from the abolition of the section 47 power referred to above, it might be expected that the Guidance would offer clarity as to the way forward. As Luke Clements says, the Guidance should be 'assured, authoritative and clear.' In fact,

> *" ... it is none of these: it does not 'guide' and in a number of respects it is materially defective. A number of commentators have noted that the safeguarding section is the least satisfactory: Dr Lucy Series suggesting that the original 2014 Statutory Guidance lacked 'legal literacy' – and the revisions in the 2016 version do little to address these failings."*
>
> *(Briefing on the Care Act, 1st edition)*

Unlike the Social Services and Well-Being (Wales) Act 2014, an inability to 'keep safe' is not in itself an eligible need. The issue is not addressed by the guidance either. The obligation for local authorities to protect vulnerable adults stems from Human Rights law – see for example **X & Y v Hounslow LBC [2009] EWCA Civ 286.** This may mean that there is a disjunction between safeguarding and the right to services.

7. Gaining access in an emergency

This is largely common to England and Wales and is dealt with in Part D.

8. Advocacy

Section 67 of the Act provides for a statutory independent advocacy scheme. The Statutory Guidance says that the issue is one that needs to be considered at the earliest stages.

Subsection 2 provides:-

> *"(2) The authority must, if the condition in subsection (4) is met, arrange for a person who is independent of the authority (an "independent advocate") to be available to represent and support the individual for the purpose of facilitating the individual's involvement ..."*

The condition to be met is set out in subsection (4).

> *"(4) The condition is that the local authority considers that, were an independent advocate not to be available, the individual would experience substantial difficulty in doing one or more of the following—*
> *(a) understanding relevant information;*
> *(b) retaining that information;*
> *(c) using or weighing that information as part of the process of being involved;*
> *(d) communicating the individual's views, wishes or feelings (whether by talking, using sign language or any other means)."*

There is a caveat in subsection (5). The duty does not arise if there is a non-professional person whom the authority believes would be an appropriate person to represent and support the individual for the purpose of facilitating the individual's involvement.

In **R (SG) v Haringey LBC [2015] EWHC 2579 (Admin)**, the failure to appoint an independent advocate (under the provisions for appointment contained in Section 67(2) of the **Care Act 2014**) for a vulnerable adult who spoke no English, was illiterate, and suffered from PTSD, insomnia, depression and anxiety, rendered the assessment unlawful.

There is no directly equivalent provision in the **Social Services and Well-Being (Wales) Act 2014,** but the Code of Practice for Part 10 of the Act (Advocacy) makes clear that local authorities **must** arrange for the provision of an independent professional advocate when a person can only overcome the barrier(s) to participate fully in the assessment, care and support planning, review and safeguarding processes with assistance from an appropriate individual, but there is no appropriate individual available.

9. Human Rights Act protection

For the purposes of the **Human Rights Act 1998**, where care or support is arranged by a local authority, or is paid for by the local authority where the care or support is provided by a registered care provider, the care provider is deemed to be a public authority, whether the care or support is provided in a residential setting or anywhere else. Section 73 of the **Care Act 2014**, which in this respect is applicable to Wales as well, says:-

> *(1) This section applies where—*
> *... (b) in Wales, a person registered under Part 2 of the Care Standards Act 2000 provides care and support to an adult, or support to a carer, in the course of providing—*
> *(i) personal care in a place where the adult receiving the personal care is living when the personal care is provided, or*
> *(ii) residential accommodation together with nursing or personal care;*
> *...*
> *(2) The provider is to be taken for the purposes of section 6(3)(b) of the Human Rights Act 1998 (acts of public authorities) to be exercising a function of a public nature in providing the care or support, if the requirements of subsection (3) are met.*
>
> *(3) The requirements are that—*

(a) the care or support is arranged by an authority listed in column 1 of the Table below, or paid for (directly or indirectly, and in whole or in part) by such an authority, and
(b) the authority arranges or pays for the care or support under a provision listed in the corresponding entry in column 2 of the Table.

10. Choice of accommodation

One of the principles of the previous legislation which remains is the choice of accommodation principle. Details are in Annex A to the Statutory Guidance and the **Care and Support and Aftercare (Choice of Accommodation) Regulations 2014 SI 2014/2670**. The regulations permit P to choose his or her own accommodation provided that:-

- The preferred accommodation is the same as that specified in P's care and support plan;
- It is suitable to P's needs;
- It is available, and
- If not provided by the local authority, the provider agrees to provide it on the local authority's terms.

This does mean that, in practice, the extent of the choice is limited by the amount which the local authority is prepared to pay.

11. Section 117 Mental Health Act 1983

Section 117 provides for after care services for patients discharged from a treatment section of the Act (i.e. section 3 or its criminal equivalents). Under the community care regime which predated the **Care Act 2014**, section 117 was a designated community care duty, and fell within the categories of services for which the local authority was obliged to carry out an assessment under section 47 of the **NHS & Community Care**

Act 1990. With the repeal of that statute, section 117 remains as a freestanding duty on the providers of care.

Because the **Care Act 2014** does not include a duty or a power to assess for services under sec 117, the former duty to assess under sec 47 of the **NHS & Community Care Act 1990** has survived the general repeal of old community care statutes, and therefore remains in place as the route to sec 117 services. It follows that the **Care Act 2014** duties regarding assessment and meeting the need do not apply to sec 117 cases.

The operative part of Sec 117 reads:-

> *117 After-care*
>
> *(1) This section applies to persons who are detained under section 3 above, or admitted to a hospital in pursuance of a hospital order made under section 37 above, or transferred to a hospital in pursuance of a hospital direction made under section 45A above or a transfer direction made under section 47 or 48 above, and then cease to be detained and (whether or not immediately after so ceasing) leave hospital.*
>
> *(2) It shall be the duty of the clinical commissioning group ... and of the local social services authority to provide or arrange for the provision of, in co-operation with relevant voluntary agencies, after-care services for any person to whom this section applies until such time as the clinical commissioning group ... and the local social services authority are satisfied that the person concerned is no longer in need of such services; but they shall not be so satisfied in the case of a community patient while he remains such a patient.*

Section 75 of the **Care Act 2014** introduces some clarifications of section 117 in respect of responsibilities and ordinary residence, and also provides a definition of services. The "local social services authority" is the authority for the area where the patient was resident immediately before his or her admission to hospital. Section 40 of the **Care Act 2014**, which covers disputes about ordinary residence, extends to a dispute as to which authority is responsible in the event of such a dispute.

Section 75 amends section 117 by introducing the following definitions. "After-care services" means:-

> "*... services which have both of the following purposes—*
> *(a) meeting a need arising from or related to the person's mental disorder; and*
> *(b) reducing the risk of a deterioration of the person's mental condition (and, accordingly, reducing the risk of the person requiring admission to a hospital again for treatment for mental disorder).*"

A new section 117A is added to the 1983 Act which provides for regulations to permit a degree of choice for a person who is being accommodated under the section, and also to confirm that those people caught by the section can top up their own care and support packages (unlike other recipients of community care; see below).

The Care Act Guidance makes only limited provision for carers of people detained under the **Mental Health Act 1983**. At paragraph 6.76 it provides:

> "*A local authority may carry out a needs or carer's assessment jointly with another body carrying out any other assessment ... provided that person agrees. ... . An integrated approach may ... include putting processes in place to ensure that the person is referred for other assessments such as an assessment for after-care needs under the Mental Health Act 1983.*"

And in the Care Planning section it provides, at paragraph 10.9, in the context of a care plan meeting the needs identified by sections 18-20 of the Care Act, that

> *Where a local authority is required to meet needs under section 117 of the Mental Health Act 1983 this chapter should be read in conjunction with chapter 34 of the "Mental Health Act 1983 Code*

of Practice" [2014] (on the Care Programme Approach) and "Refocusing the Care Programme Approach" [2008].

It should also be noted that the Code of Practice for the Mental Health Act makes no reference to the position of carers of those covered by the **Mental Health Act 1983**, even though it is clearly the case that they are covered.

CHAPTER FOUR: PAYING FOR CARE IN ENGLAND

1. The Dilnot Report

Payment for social care has been a political hot potato for many years. The latest attempt to address the issue was the report of the Commission on Funding of Care and Support (the Dilnot Commission) in July 2011. The Dilnot Commission was set up in July 2010 by the coalition Government, tasked with making recommendations for changes to the funding of care and support in England.

Prior to the coming into force of the **Care Act 2014**, payment by individuals or by local authorities for placements in residential care was governed by sec 22 of the **National Assistance Act 1948**, and by the **National Assistance (Assessment of Resources) Regulations 1992 SI 1992/2977**. The system of charging for domiciliary services was contained in guidance (**Fairer Charging Policies for Home Care and other non-residential Social Services**). Authorities were expected to follow the guidance, and this included an expectation that they would not include measures which were less generous than those governing the mandatory system of payment for residential care. Effectively, therefore, the payment regime for all social care provision in England referred to the 1948 Act legislation. As also indicated below, a different system for domiciliary care charges had grown up in Wales, although much of the thinking behind the English system also applied to the Welsh system.

Among Dilnot's recommendations were that the government should set a cap on an individual's contribution towards his or her own care costs over their lifetime, and that the government should meet any costs in excess of that. The range suggested for the cap was between £25,000 and £50,000, although the Commission itself suggested that £35,000 would be a suitable figure.

Dilnot proposed that people should in any event pay towards their living costs such as food and accommodation, but this again would be subject to a cap of between £7,000 and £10,000 a year. The upper capital limit should be raised from £23,250 to £100,000.

The report proposed that those entering adulthood with a need for care and support should be eligible for free state support immediately, rather than being subject to a means test. Those whose need for care develops above the age of 40 should be subject to a tiered cap, starting at £10,000 for a 40 year old, £20,000 for a 50 year old, £30,000 for a 60 year old and £35,000 for a 65 year old.

The report recommended that its proposal should be implemented from 2013, and anticipated a white paper at Easter 2012. The total expected cost of full implementation of Dilnot's proposals would have been in the region of £1.7bn a year.

2. How the Care Act 2014 approached Dilnot

The Act provided that payment for both residential and domiciliary care should be calculated on the same basis. There were also two principal provisions of Dilnot which were incorporated in the new scheme, with a view that they would be implemented from April 2016.

The provisions were:-

- The implementation of a lifetime cap on care costs, and
- An increase in the capital limit, which is the figure below which a person will be entitled to some contribution towards their care costs.

However, as noted below, these proposals have been postponed and will not now be implemented before April 2020. The description of the scheme which follows, therefore, takes no account of the care cap or of the proposed increases to the capital limits, particularly in view of recent assertions by politicians of different approaches to the problem.

3. Funding of Care and Support

3.1 Charging Legislation

Where a person is placed in residential accommodation or is provided with domiciliary services which are funded by the local authority, the authority is entitled to make a charge if they so determine (**Care Act 2014,** sec 14). Note that they do not have to do so. The charges are based on a national statutory scheme and are covered by the **Care and Support (Charging and Assessment of Resources) Regulations 2014 SI 2014/2672,** and by the Care and Support Statutory Guidance, particularly chapters 8 and 9, and annexes A to E.

The Guidance includes a set of principles for local authorities to take into account in determining charges, namely:-

- Ensure people are not charged more than it is reasonable for them to pay;
- Be comprehensive, to reduce variations;
- Be clear and transparent;
- Promote wellbeing and social inclusion, and "support the vision of" personalisation, independence, choice and control;
- Support carers to look after their own needs and to care effectively;
- Be person-focussed;
- Apply the charging rules equally and minimise the differences and anomalies between individual care settings;
- Encourage people to take up, or to stay in, employment, education or training, or plan for the future costs of their doing so;
- Be sustainable for local authorities in the long term.

The **Care Act 2014** introduces the concept of "light touch assessments" – where it is clear that a person does, or does not, meet the financial limits (e.g. a single person placed permanently in residential accommodation leaving an unoccupied house which they own) the authority need not carry out a detailed means test. Generally the individual must consent.

The means test is similar to, but not identical to, the means tested schemes used for benefits. In particular it should be noted that the means of a resident are not aggregated with those of his or her partner, unlike the position in means tested welfare benefits. However, care should be taken if it is felt that a person can therefore dispose of all or part of his or her capital by giving it to their partner, as the notional capital rules will apply. Both the method of dealing with property of couples, and the notional capital rules, are considered in Part D.

Where a local authority places a person in residential accommodation, and that person lacks capacity, the local authority may not disclaim their liability to pay the fees on the basis that the resident has enough capital and income to be regarded as a self-funder; see **Aster Healthcare v the Estate of Mohammed Shafi [2014] EWCA Civ 1350.**

3.2 Current capital limits

The capital limits for England are as follows:-

Lower Capital Limit	£14,250
Upper Capital Limit	£23,250

If the claimant has capital above the upper limit, he or she pays the full cost of their care. If he or she has capital below that level, but above the lower level, he or she is treated as receiving income from the capital, which is calculated according to a tariff.

The tariff operates by deeming anyone with capital above the lower limit, but below the upper limit, to be receiving income from that capital. The rate at which income is deemed to be received, and hence the amount which is allocated as part of the person's income, is £1 for every £250 or part of £250 above the lower limit.

So, for example, Doris has £17,000 capital. She is between the two limits, so she will be deemed to receive income from her capital. The first £14,250 is ignored. She has excess capital of £2,750, so she is deemed to receive £11 per week from it. Any actual receipt of income from the capital is disregarded.

3.3 Contribution for those below the capital limits – means test

Certain services must be provided free of charge. These include:-

- The provision of community equipment (aids and adaptations);
- Intermediate care and reablement services, for a period of six weeks;
- Services provided to someone with variant Creutzfeldt-Jakob Disease.

In addition, services provided under the **Mental Health Act 1983** section 117 may not be charged for (**R (Stennett) v Manchester City Council** [2002] **2 AC 1127**).

There is a minimum income guarantee. Where a person is a permanent or temporary resident in a residential care home, the amount is £24.90 per week. Where the person is not a resident, the guaranteed amount is calculated by reference to their personal circumstances. In a similar way to income support calculations, the amount consists of a personal amount for the adult concerned, plus a premium where they are a member of a couple, over pension age, or disabled, plus a fixed amount for any child for whom they are responsible. The amounts are as set out in the table below.

Minimum weekly income

	Personal amount	For each child	Entitled to disability premium	Entitled to enhanced disability premium	Carer
Single person aged 18-24	72.40	83.65	40.35	19.70	43.25
Single person aged 25 to PC age*	91.40	83.65	40.35	19.70	43.25
Single person aged PC age +	189.00	83.65	40.35	19.70	43.25
Lone parent aged 18+	91.40	83.65	40.35	19.70	43.25
Member of a couple aged 18+ (one or both)	71.80	83.65	28.75	14.15	43.25
Member of a couple over PC age (one or both)	144.30	83.65	28.75	14.15	43.25

*PC Age = pension credit age, which is the age at which a woman may claim a state retirement pension. This age is currently being increased in monthly instalments from 60 to 65, and is due to reach 65 in 2018.

4. Residential accommodation

4.1 Temporary or permanent residence

Care needs to be taken to ensure that all parties are clear as to whether the occupancy is temporary or permanent, as different funding rules apply.

A person who is placed in a residential care home as part of an intermediate care package is entitled to the accommodation free of charge.

A temporary resident is one whose stay is not expected to exceed 52 weeks. It should be recorded on the care plan that the stay is temporary. The local authority is required to disregard the value of any house which the resident is trying to sell as part of an attempt to downsize; or to which they intend to return (Schedule 2 Paragraph 1).

4.2 The 12 week Property Disregard

Where someone becomes a permanent resident, the value of any house they own is normally disregarded for the first 12 weeks.

If a permanent resident leaves residential care before the expiry of the 12 weeks, but later returns, then the balance of the 12 weeks will apply provided that they re-entered during the first 52 weeks. If re-entry is more than 52 weeks later, then the disregard applies again.

4.3 Deferred Payment Agreements (DPAs)

Deferred Payment Agreements, previously covered in guidance, became statutory with the introduction of the **Care Act**. The statutory provisions are to be found in sections 34 to 36. The regulations are the **Care and Support (Deferred Payment Agreements) Regulations 2014 SI 2014/2671** and the topic is covered in Chapter 9 of the Guidance.

Local authorities are obliged to offer DPAs to people who meet the criteria. The criteria are:-

(a) the person must have needs which are to be met by the provision of care in a care home. This should comply with choice of accommodation regulations and care and support planning guidance and so take reasonable account of a person's preferences;

(b) they must have capital of £23,250 or less excluding their home; and

(c) the home must not be disregarded.

The authority may refuse to offer a DPA where:-

(a) they are unable to secure a first charge on the person's property; or

(b) the person is seeking a top up; and/or

(c) they do not agree to the terms and conditions of the agreement, for example a requirement to insure and maintain the property.

Authorities can recover administration charges for setting up and administering a DPA, and can charge interest from the first day on any amount deferred. The amount of the interest charge is subject to a national maximum which is set every year on 1st January and 1st July.

A deferred payment agreement can be terminated in three ways:

(a) at any time by the individual, or someone acting on their behalf, by repaying the full amount due (this can happen during a person's lifetime or when the agreement is terminated through the DPA holder's death);

(b) when the property (or security) is sold and the authority is repaid; or

(c) when the person dies and the amount is repaid to the LA from their estate.

5. General provisions about the means test

Because the means test outlined above makes provision for the assessment of the assets of an individual, it is quite common for someone with assets (usually but not invariably in the form of a house) to seek to protect them from assessment by giving them away, or by setting up some form of trust. All such arrangements are subject to the deprivation rule, which can be stated broadly as saying that someone who seeks to get their care fees paid by depriving themselves of any asset may be treated as if they still possessed the asset, i.e. they would be charged for the cost of their care anyway. This rule, being common to both England and Wales, is discussed further in Part D of this book.

6. Personalisation and direct payments

6.1 Introduction

Personalisation is a social care approach which has been described by the Department of Health as meaning that "every person who receives support, whether provided by statutory services or funded by themselves, will have choice and control over the shape of that support in all care settings". It has been mainstream Government policy since 2007 that it would be appropriate to move towards the "personalisation" of public services. Although the move towards personalisation was formerly contained in guidance, not in legislation, the **Care Act 2014** made this a statutory requirement under sections 26 and 28.

Sections 31 to 33 of the **Care Act 2014** provide for the payment to an adult of sums (direct payments) to enable him or her to buy in their own care, and make different provisions as to how this is to be done depending on whether the adult has, or lacks, capacity. See *https://www.gov.uk/apply-direct-payments*. The Department of Health publication "Independence, choice and risk: A Guide to Best Practice in Decision Making", which was published in May 2007, contains useful information, and is still available via the Social Care Institute for Excellence at http://www.scie-socialcareonline.org.uk/independence-choice-and-risk-a-guide-to-best-practice-in-supported-decision-making/r/a11G00000017qauIAA

The paperwork and administration required to operate direct payments, particularly the obligations arising if the service user becomes an employer, should not be underestimated. A number of charities and support organisations offer advice and assistance on managing direct payments schemes. Useful guidance including support for employment, together with factsheets on areas such as PAYE, registration with the Inland Revenue as an employer and the impact of working time regulations on night-time care can be found via the charity The Rowan Foundation – *www.therowan.org* .

Some people will relish the opportunity to have control over their care services; however abuse or exploitation could occur without proper safeguards. Any care workers employed on behalf of the local authority through a domiciliary agency to deliver personal care in a service user's home should be checked before being permitted to provide any care services in a domiciliary setting. If the service user contracts directly with an individual to provide care no such checks are necessary nor is there any guarantee that the person has been fully trained to deliver the appropriate level of care.

The Direct Payments scheme only relates to the social service element of any care package and cannot be used where there is a partnership arrangement involving the provision of healthcare services. For direct payments in health, see https://www.england.nhs.uk/wp-content/uploads/2017/06/guid-dirct-paymnt.pdf

Direct payments cannot be used to buy anything for which the local authority would not be responsible, e.g. providing NHS level care, and they should not be used as a substitute for a disabled facilities grant.

It would be up to the local authority to decide on the amount of the direct payment but the direct payments legislation requires that it must be sufficient to the council's estimate of the reasonable costs of securing provision of the services concerned.

Direct payments should be sufficient to enable the user lawfully to secure a service of a standard that the council considers is reasonable to fulfil the needs for the service to which the payment relates. There should be no limit on the maximum or minimum amounts of direct payments, either in the amount of care that it is intended to be purchased, or on the value of the direct payments.

There is no obligation upon the local authority to pay for the service user's preferred option if the cost exceeds the local authority's estimate of the reasonable costs of securing the care and it can be established that the service can be secured in a more cost effective manner.

The local authority does have the right to require repayment of direct payments if they are not satisfied that the money has been used to secure the provision of services to which it relates. The local authority may also decide that the conditions attached to the direct payments being made are not being met and if so they can stop the direct payment, but of course the requirement to provide services does not cease and the local authority will still be under an obligation to provide the services.

6.2 Determining the amount payable

The amount payable by way of a direct payment is normally calculated by the local authority using a standard formula, which is known as the Resource Allocation System or RAS. This is lawful provided that the local authority does not slavishly follow the results of the formula, but treats it as a starting point, and provided that they take care fully to explain to the service user how they have reached their decisions.

As a generalisation, it may be stated that the use of a formula is lawful provided its results are treated as an indication of the amount, and not as being absolutely binding. These matters have been considered by the courts in two principal cases; at first instance in **R (Savva) v Royal Borough of Kensington & Chelsea [2010] EWHC 414 (Admin)**, and by the Supreme Court in **R (KM) v Cambridgeshire County Council [2012] UKSC 23.** Those seeking a detailed view of the court's approach to the RAS are directed to these cases which are not considered further here.

7. The postponed Care Act 2014 proposals for 2016

These provisions were included in the Care Act with the intention that they should apply in England from April 2016. In the event, however, not least because of the persuasion of local authorities, the Government announced that both these measures will be postponed until (at the earliest) April 2020. The provisions affected are the care cap, and the increase in the capital limits.

The proposed rate for the care cap was:-

- Where eligible needs exist at the age of 18 – zero
- Where eligible needs arise during working age – to be decided but less than £72,000
- Pension age or over - £72,000.

This would have meant that, once the amount actually paid by an individual reached the level of the care cap, they would no longer have to pay for their care. They would continue to have to pay other charges.

For those in residential care, it should therefore be borne in mind that only the care cost part of their care home fee would have gone towards the care cap. This in turn would have been based on what the local authority would normally pay, rather than what the resident actually paid. The resident who reached the care cap would nevertheless be expected to continue to pay other charges; however, the charge for board and lodging would have been capped at £230 a week (2016 figures).

The proposals for the capital limit (also postponed) were as follows:-

New capital limit for care home residents

- Upper limit £118,000
- Lower limit £17,000

New capital limit for care at home

- Upper limit £27,000
- Lower limit £17,000

There would be a tariff income applied at the same rate as now, i.e. £1 for every £250. This would mean that someone in residential care with £100,000 capital would pay from their tariff income alone £332 a week. They may also have other income which will be taken into account. Because they are local authority funded, they would also lose any entitlement to Disability Living Allowance, Personal Independence Payments or Attendance Allowance after 28 days.

PART C – THE LAW IN WALES

CHAPTER ONE: THE STRUCTURE OF THE SOCIAL SERVICES AND WELL-BEING (WALES) ACT 2014

1. General principles

The Act repeals almost all of the principal adult care statutes, including the **National Assistance Act 1948** and the **NHS & Community Care Act 1990**.

As well as the Act itself, there are numerous regulations and Codes of Practice. Generally there is a Code to each Chapter of the Act. The Codes are issued under sec 145 which requires authorities to "act in accordance with any relevant requirement contained in a Code" and to have regard to any guidelines in the Code. There is no Code for Part 7 of the Act, which covers safeguarding, and instead there is statutory guidance issued under sec 131.

Probably the best links for further information are the Care Council for Wales (www.ccwales.org.uk/the-act/) and the material produced by Luke Clements which can be found at www.lukeclements.co.uk .

2. The general duties of the authority

The Act contains a general duty (in Section 5) to promote the 'well-being' of people 'in need' and carers. Well-being is defined as follows, in section 2:

> *(2) "Well-being", in relation to a person, means well-being in relation to any of the following—*
> *(a) physical and mental health and emotional well-being;*
> *(b) protection from abuse and neglect;*
> *(c) education, training and recreation;*
> *(d) domestic, family and personal relationships;*
> *(e) contribution made to society;*

(f) securing rights and entitlements;
(g) social and economic well-being;
(h) suitability of living accommodation.

(3) In relation to a child, "well-being" also includes—
(a) physical, intellectual, emotional, social and behavioural development;
(b) "welfare" as that word is interpreted for the purposes of the Children Act 1989.

(4) In relation to an adult, "well-being" also includes—
(a) control over day to day life;
(b) participation in work.

The word 'choice' does not appear, although 'control' does.

Section 6 requires a person carrying out functions under the Act to:

(a) in so far as is reasonably practicable, ascertain and have regard to the individual's views, wishes and feelings,
(b) have regard to the importance of promoting and respecting the dignity of the individual,
(c) have regard to the characteristics, culture and beliefs of the individual (including, for example, language), and
(d) have regard to the importance of providing appropriate support to enable the individual to participate in decisions that affect him or her to the extent that is appropriate in the circumstances, particularly where the individual's ability to communicate is limited for any reason.

In the case of an adult, the person who is assessing (etc.) is also required to have regard to the importance of beginning with the presumption that the adult is best placed to judge his or her own well-being, and to the importance of promoting independence. In the case of a child, the person must have regard to the importance of promoting the upbringing of the child by his or her family, insofar as this is consistent with promoting the child's well-being, and also must where possible take into account the views, wishes and feelings of a person with parental responsibility for the child.

The right to independent living, which is protected by **Article 19** of the **UN Convention on the Rights of Persons with Disabilities**, is specifically referred to in Section 6(3)(b), unlike the English statute, which relies on a statement in Parliament by the Minister. There is also a specific reference to the UN Convention in Quality Standard 1 of the **Code of Practice in Relation to Measuring Social Services Performance**. Given the willingness of the courts to have regard to the Convention (see for example **Burnip v Birmingham City Council [2012] EWCA Civ 629**, and **R (Bracking) v SSWP** [2013] **EWCA Civ 1345**, this may encourage use of the Convention to secure rights under the Act. See also **Mathieson v Secretary of State for Work and Pensions** [2015] **UKSC** 47.

There is a potential issue with the statement set out above in section 2(3)(b), which states that, in the case of a child, "well-being" also includes welfare as interpreted in the Children Act 1989. The Children Act does not in fact define welfare from the point of view of the local authority, although it does provide (in section 1(3) of the Children Act 1989) a "welfare checklist". It has been judicially suggested that the terms are synonymous: see **Re G** [2012] **EWCA Civ 1233** at para 26.

The status of the English duty towards the well-being of a service user, which is likely to be at least persuasive in Wales, was considered in the cases of **R (Davey) v Oxfordshire County Council** [2017] **EWHC** 354, and **R (JF) v Merton LBC** [2017] **EWHC 1519 (Admin)** which are considered in Part D below.

3. Definitions

The definition of disability contained in section 29 **National Assistance Act 1948** has been repealed. The former principle of attempting to define a person as meeting a definition of disability (or not) ought to have disappeared. However, the term survives in the new Act; rights attach to a person who cares for a "disabled child". Section 3(5) gives the term 'disabled' the same meaning as in the **Equality Act 2010**.

A carer is no longer defined as someone who provides or intends to provide substantial care on a regular basis. Section 3(4) of the Act defines a carer as a person who provides or intends to provide care for an adult or disabled child. This is subject to the exclusions of paid carers and those who carry out care as voluntary work (although the local authority may determine that it would be appropriate to treat a volunteer as a carer in certain cases), and those who are in custody after conviction of a criminal offence.

4. Other local authority duties

Local authorities and local health boards are placed under general duties jointly to assess the need for care and support, and for support for carers, by section 14. By section 15 they are required to provide a range of services which, among other things, will contribute towards preventing or delaying the development of people's needs for care and support; will reduce the needs for care and support; and will promote the upbringing of children by their families, where that is consistent with the well-being of children.

Under section 16, there is a duty to promote the development of social enterprises and similar bodies. This is a contrast to the English Act, which requires a local authority to promote a range of private sector providers. The thinking behind both provisions would seem to be the same, namely the requirement not to put all eggs in one basket in terms of providers. This follows the collapse of the care home provider Southern Cross Healthcare in 2011. The duty is expanded upon in **The Social Services and Well-being (Wales) Act 2014 (Social Enterprise, Co-operative and Third Sector (Wales) Regulations 2015 SI 2015/1500 (W.172)**, and by Part 2 of the Code of Practice.

Section 17 requires local authorities to provide people in need and their carers with information about the care and support that is available in their area. This includes information about what is available, how it can be accessed, and how concerns and complaints can be raised. Local authorities and LHBs are also required to publish a strategy for ensuring that there is a suitable level of services to meet local needs.

CHAPTER TWO: ASSESSMENT IN WALES

1. The Single Assessment

An **assessment** is the process of considering a person's circumstances and making a decision about whether they need care and support to help them live their day-to-day lives. The assessment for care and support is usually carried out by a social worker, and will consider the presenting needs as well as the person's other circumstances.

Under the former system, following the determination of needs, the local authority was required to consider what eligible services to provide. They did so using an eligibility framework, which was laid down in guidance. This required the setting of four categories of need (critical, substantial, moderate and low) and a decision as to which categories services would be provided. An individual service user would then be assessed as belonging in a particular category and this would determine their entitlement (or otherwise) to services. Which needs were eligible for services was therefore a matter for the authority under the guidance; but once the service user was assessed as eligible, the authority had a duty to provide the service (see Lord Wilson in **R (KM) v Cambridgeshire County Council, [2012] UKSC 23**). The consequence of non-standard eligibility criteria was that what constitutes eligible needs varied from one area to another. It is also important to note that local authorities were able to determine to which categories of people they planned to provide support by reference to their own financial situation, i.e. they might have provided services to those in all four categories, or to only three, or two, or even one. Under the previous scheme, most authorities were providing services to those in the critical and substantial categories. See **R v Gloucestershire County Council ex parte Barry [1997] 2 WLR 459.**

The Act creates (in section 19) a single duty for local authorities to carry out assessments in order to determine whether an adult has needs for care and support. It says:

(1) Where it appears to a local authority that an adult may have needs for care and support, the authority must assess—
(a) whether the adult does have needs for care and support, and
(b) if the adult does, what those needs are.

The appearance of need is sufficient to trigger the duty, and an application is not necessary.

Section 19 requires that the assessment:

- must be of the adult's needs and the outcomes they want to achieve;
- must be provided to all people who appear to have some need for care and support, and therefore should not consider unrelated factors such as a person's finances;
- must not consider whether the local authority thinks the person will be eligible for services (see **R v Bristol CC ex parte Penfold (1998) 1 CCLR. 315**); and
- must be carried out with involvement from the adult and, where appropriate, their carer or someone else they nominate.

Unlike the previous legislation, there is no categorisation of individuals according to type (so for example the definition of a disabled person, formerly in section 29 of the **National Assistance Act 1948**, disappears). Nor is there a list of potential services, unlike that in section 2 of the **Chronically Sick and Disabled Persons Act 1970**.

Under section 20, an adult may refuse an assessment and the local authority's duty will be discharged, except in three situations:

- the adult lacks capacity but someone else can make the decision for them;
- the adult lacks capacity and has no-one else to make the decision, but it is in their best interests;

- the adult is or may be experiencing abuse or neglect, or be at risk of doing so.

The duty will however be reinstated if the person requests an assessment, or if their circumstances change.

The assessment process is governed by the **Care and Support (Assessment) (Wales) Regulations 2015 SI 2015/1305 (W.111)**. Part 3 of the Code of Practice specifies the minimum content of the record of the assessment. The Guidance states at para 63 that there should be a comprehensive analysis of five key elements:

- The person's circumstances;
- Their personal outcomes;
- The barriers to achieving those outcomes;
- The risks to them or to others if those outcomes are not achieved; and
- The person's strengths and capabilities.

Part 3 also makes clear (at para 80) that when undertaking an assessment the authority "must identify all presenting needs including those which would be deemed as eligible **if a carer was not meeting those needs**" (emphasis added). This is different from the position in England. Under the equivalent English regulations, the determination of an adult's eligible needs is made without taking into account any support which is being provided by a carer. The English Guidance says

> *6.15 During the assessment, local authorities must consider all of the adult's care and support needs, regardless of any support being provided by a carer. Where the adult has a carer, information on the care that they are providing can be captured during assessment, but it must not influence the eligibility determination.*

In other words, eligibility in England is not affected by care actually supplied. This is commonly referred to as a "carer blind assessment". In Wales, however, care provided by a willing carer is not ignored for eligibility purposes, but the information is intended to enable the authority to respond when the carer becomes unable or unwilling to continue to meet the needs. This is surely wrong; it means that the assessment confuses needs with whether or not they are met.

2. Assessment of children

Sections 21 to 23 govern the assessment of children in need. This is an addition to the previous law, which dealt (in section 17 **Children Act 1989**) with children in need, but did not provide any explicit statutory duty to carry out an assessment. There is now such a duty, which is similar to that for an adult. The appearance of need is sufficient to trigger the duty.

Section 21 requires that the assessment:

- must be of the child's needs and the outcomes they want to achieve, and that those with parental responsibility for the child wish to achieve for him or her;
- must be provided to all children who appear to have some need for care and support, and therefore should not consider unrelated factors such as the child's finances, or the finances of those with parental responsibility for the child;
- must not consider whether the local authority thinks the person will be eligible for care and support, or support; and
- must be carried out with involvement from the child and anyone with parental responsibility for him or her.

Section 21(7) creates a presumption that a child who is disabled (i.e. who has a disability recognised under the **Equality Act 2010**) has needs for additional or substitute care and support. The same provisions as to the identification of needs which are being met by a carer apply to a child as to an adult.

Sections 22-23 cover refusal of an assessment. Under section 22, if the child is aged 16 or 17 and has capacity, they can themselves refuse an assessment. If they lack capacity, and if a person with parental responsibility, or someone authorised under the **Mental Capacity Act 2005**, refuses an assessment on their behalf, the duty is similarly discharged. The exceptions to these rules are where the refusal is made by a child, or a person with parental responsibility, who lacks capacity; or where a refusal by a person with parental responsibility is not in the child's best interests; or the child is or may be experiencing abuse or neglect, or be at risk of doing so.

Where a child is under 16, section 23 applies. The child may themselves refuse if they are Gillick competent, or a person with parental responsibility may refuse on their behalf. The exceptions are where it is the person with parental responsibility who makes the refusal, but he or she lacks capacity; or the refusal is contrary to the wishes of a Gillick competent child; or the refusal is inconsistent with the child's well-being, or the child is or may be experiencing abuse or neglect, or be at risk of doing so. "Gillick competent" refers to the child's ability to give consent or not to his or her own care, after the case of **Gillick v West Norfolk and Wisbech Area Health Authority and the Department of Health and Social Security** **[1986] AC 112.**

3. Assessment of carers

Carers' assessments are covered by sections 24 to 27. Section 24 imposes the duty; section 25 covers refusal by a carer of full age and capacity; section 26 covers refusal by a carer aged 16 or 17, and section 27 covers a refusal by or on behalf of a carer under 16.

The Act creates a single duty for local authorities to undertake a 'carer's assessment'. This replaces the previous law, firstly by removing the requirement that the carer must be providing "a substantial amount of care on a regular basis", and secondly by imposing the duty to assess. This will mean more carers are able to access an assessment, and that the duty is comparable to that for the people they support.

The duty to assess is again triggered by the appearance of a need, which in the case of a carer is a need for support. The aim of the assessment is to consider the impact of caring on the carer. Section 24(4) tells the authority what to consider:-

> *(4) In carrying out a needs assessment under this section, the local authority must—*
> *(a) assess the extent to which the carer is able, and will continue to be able, to provide care for the person for whom the carer provides or intends to provide care,*
> *(b) assess the extent to which the carer is willing, and will continue to be willing, to do so,*
> *(c) in the case of a carer who is an adult, seek to identify the outcomes that the carer wishes to achieve,*
> *(d) in the case of a carer who is a child, seek to identify the outcomes that—*
> *(i) the carer wishes to achieve, to the extent it considers appropriate having regard to the carer's age and understanding,*
> *(ii) the persons with parental responsibility for the carer wish to achieve in relation to the carer, to the extent it considers appropriate having regard to the need to promote the carer's well-being, and*
> *(iii) persons specified in regulations (if any) wish to achieve in relation to the carer,*

If both the carer and the person they care for agree, a joint assessment of both their needs can be undertaken (section 28). A combined assessment cannot be imposed, except in the case of a child under 16 where a combined assessment would be consistent with the child's well-being.

The assessment should seek to establish not just the carer's needs for support but also the sustainability of the carer's role.

There is no distinction between the rights of adult carers and of young carers, except for minor differences such as seeking to ascertain the outcomes which a young carer wishes "to the extent" that it is "appropriate having regard to the carer's age and understanding", and also bringing into account the views of the parent or parents and the extent to which the tasks of a carer are consistent with the young person's well-being. The assessment should also take account of the child's own developmental needs.

4. Entitlement to Care and Support

After conducting the needs assessment, the local authority is then required to determine whether the person has eligible needs, using an eligibility framework which is now statutory and no longer contained in guidance. The previous categories of need ('critical', 'substantial', 'moderate', and 'low') have disappeared, and there is now a national standard for eligibility.

The intention was to address the previous situation of different statutes and different levels of entitlement for care and support. For example, the legal test for residential accommodation was significantly different from the test for domiciliary care. The intention was also to remove some of the anomalies in the legislation which created different entitlements for different groups of people.

The Act sets out to create a single, consistent route to establishing an entitlement to care and support for all adults and children. It also creates an entitlement to support for carers, on a similar basis.

Once the assessment is completed, the authority is required by the **Care and Support (Eligibility) (Wales) Regulations 2015 SI 2015/1578 (W.187)** to determine whether the needs which have been found also meet the eligibility criteria. If they do, then consideration moves to the provision of care and support to meet those needs.

There are four stages in determining eligibility, which generally speaking apply to all potential recipients of care or support – adults, children, and carers. These are:-

(a) **The need must arise for a specified reason**. The specified reasons are:-

- Adult in need (reg 3) – the need arises from their physical or mental ill-health, age, disability, dependence on drugs or alcohol, or other similar circumstances;
- Child in need (reg 4) – the needs are as for an adult (above) or if the needs are unmet, they are likely to have an adverse effect on the child's development;
- Carer (reg 5) – the need arises as a result of providing care for an adult in need (as described above) or for a disabled child.

(b) **The need must relate to a set of standard tasks**. These are:-

- Ability to carry out basic self-care or domestic routines
- Ability to communicate
- Protection from abuse or neglect
- Involvement in work, education, learning or leisure activities
- Maintenance or development of family or other significant personal relationships
- Development and maintenance of social relationships and involvement in the community.

"Basic self-care" is defined in regulation 1. It consists of:-

> "*Tasks that a person carries out as part of daily life including*
> - *Eating and drinking*

- *Maintaining personal hygiene*
- *Getting up and getting dressed*
- *Moving around the home*
- *Preparing meals*
- *Keeping the home clean, safe and hygienic"*

In addition there are two specific eligible tasks for, respectively, adults and children. For an adult the task is to be able to fulfil their caring responsibilities for a child. For a child (or a child carer) the task is to achieve developmental goals.

(c) **The person (and his or her parents, if s/he is a child) is not able to meet that need**, either-

- Alone, or
- With the help of others willing to provide support, or
- With the assistance of community services to which the person has access.

The effect is that, if a person is able to meet the need with the support of a carer, they are ineligible – as opposed to England where assessments are "carer blind".

(d) **The person is unlikely to achieve one or more of the personal outcomes** unless the local authority provides or arranges for care and support to meet the need.

The responsibility for determining whether the person is eligible and whether generalised services have been tried and have failed is on the assessor. The Part 4 Code says:-

> *"33. The eligibility criteria must not be used as a tool to require individuals to demonstrate they have exhausted every other possible*

> *avenue of support before becoming eligible for local authority assistance.*
>
> *34. It is the responsibility of the local authority to identify and record … how the personal outcomes will be achieved."*

It is not clear how stage 4 provides an additional test to stage 3. Unlike the English legislation, there is no requirement that an inability to meet needs (or outcomes) shall have a significant impact on the service user.

CHAPTER THREE: PROVISION OF SERVICES IN WALES

1. Ways of Meeting the Need

The requirement of the former legislation that an assessment determined whether there was a need for "services" has been repealed. The new legislation, in section 34, sets out an illustrative list of ways in which a local authority may meet needs, as follows:

> *The following are examples of the ways in which a local authority may meet needs under sections 35 to 45—*
> *(a) by arranging for a person other than the authority to provide something;*
> *(b) by itself providing something;*
> *(c) by providing something, or by arranging for something to be provided, to a person other than the person with needs for care and support (or, in the case of a carer, support).*
>
> *(2)The following are examples of what may be provided or arranged to meet needs under sections 35 to 45—*
> *(a) accommodation in a care home, children's home or premises of some other type;*
> *(b) care and support at home or in the community;*
> *(c) services, goods and facilities;*
> *(d) information and advice;*
> *(e) counselling and advocacy;*
> *(f) social work;*
> *(g) payments (including direct payments);*
> *(h) aids and adaptations;*
> *(i) occupational therapy.*

Where an individual's needs meet the criteria, there is a duty under sections 35 to 45 to ensure that their care and support needs are met, provided they are ordinarily resident in the local authority's area. Even if their capital or income exceeds the limits, there will nevertheless be a duty on the authority to meet those needs for care and support.

As well as imposing these duties, the Act also strengthens the position of a "child in need"; it converts the power to make provision for carers into a duty; and it adds a duty to meet the needs of those who, although they fail to meet the eligibility criteria, are considered to be at risk of abuse or neglect.

The primary responsibility is to those who are ordinarily resident in the local authority's area. The topic of ordinary residence is considered in Part D. Where the result of an assessment is that a person is not eligible, there are nevertheless powers to meet the needs of an adult (at section 36), a child (at section 38) and of a carer (at section 45). There is still a limitation in section 46 on meeting the needs of those who are subject to immigration control (see Part D below).

2. Duty to meet the needs of adults

This is little different to the previous law, except that the duty is extended to self-funders. The relationship with needs being met by a carer (discussed above) is explicitly stated in section 35(6) – the duty to meet the needs of an otherwise eligible adult "does not apply ... to the extent that the local authority is satisfied that those needs are being met by a carer."

The duty arises (among other circumstances) where:

> *(a) there is no charge for the care and support needed to meet those needs, or*
> *(b) there is a charge for that care and support but—*
>
> *(i) the local authority is satisfied on the basis of a financial assessment that the adult's financial resources are at or below the financial limit,*
>
> *(ii) the local authority is satisfied on the basis of a financial assessment that the adult's financial resources are above the financial limit but the adult nonetheless asks the authority to meet his or her needs, or*

> *(iii) the local authority is satisfied that the adult lacks capacity to arrange for the provision of care and support and there is no person authorised to make such arrangements under the Mental Capacity Act 2005 or otherwise in a position to do so on the adult's behalf.*

It will be noted that section 35 (4) (b) (ii) includes the duty to meet the needs of a self-funder if so requested. The incentives for a self-funder to ask the local authority to meet their needs are twofold; firstly any services (especially residential accommodation) may be obtained at the local authority rate (although the resident is nevertheless liable for the full cost of the placement and an additional charge may be levied); and if the proposals for a care cap were to proceed. However, as discussed below, plans for a care cap have been shelved for the foreseeable future.

3. Duty to meet the needs of children

Unlike the limited duty under the previous legislation, section 37 makes explicit the duty to provide all children with the care and support they are assessed as needing, or to protect them from harm.

The duty under sec 37 does not apply to children who are "looked after", for whom the Act makes detailed provisions in Part 6 (Sections 74-125). The provisions for looked after children which are found in the **Children Act 1989** (section 22) have been superseded. In addition, the effect of the Welsh legislation is to remove the definition of a child in need from section 17 of the **Children Act 1989** and replace it with the definitions of the new Act. Part 3 of the **Children Act 1989** now only applies to England.

The Act does not contain any provisions which deal with a disabled child or their carers when a young person is in transition to adulthood. It would appear that on the child attaining 18 he or she becomes an adult and the different provisions apply, without any provision for staging the transition.

4. Duty to meet the needs of adult carers and young carers

Local authorities are placed under a duty by sections 40 to 44 to meet the eligible needs of adult carers and young carers, unless they are able to produce cogent reasons for not doing so. The provisions are extremely complex, covering as they do the possible permutations of carers over or under 18; carers and people in need having or lacking capacity to agree to their care needs; carers and those for whom they are caring having assets over or under the threshold. Much of this information would have been better included in regulations.

5. Care and Support Plans

Sections 54-55 cover the duty to prepare care and support plans for those with eligible needs. Section 54 provides that everyone is entitled to a care and support plan, or (in the case of a carer) a support plan. The local authority must involve the person for whom the plan is being prepared, plus if applicable any person with parental responsibility for a child, plus if feasible the person's carer or (in the case of a carer) the person for whom s/he cares. Section 54 also contains provisions for amendment and review of the care plan. The plan must be developed in conjunction with the service user, and there must be a named individual for the service user to contact.

6. The services to be provided to meet the need

This is largely common to both jurisdictions, and is considered in Part D below.

7. People from abroad

The law on this topic is found in Section D.

8. Safeguarding

Safeguarding is covered in sections 126 to 142 of the Act. Protection from abuse and neglect is defined as a key component of well-being, and eligibility can come about because of abuse or neglect.

The duty is to safeguard a person who is at risk. This means, in the case of an adult, someone who

- is experiencing or is at risk of abuse or neglect, and
- has needs for care and support, and
- as a result of the needs is unable to protect him or herself against the abuse or neglect.

A child is at risk if s/he is experiencing (or is at risk of) abuse, neglect or other kinds of harm, and has needs for care and support, whether or not the authority is meeting them.

Abuse is defined, in section 197, as being physical, sexual, psychological, emotional or financial. Financial abuse includes

- having money stolen, or
- being defrauded, or
- being put under pressure in relation to money, or
- having money or other property misused.

Neglect is a failure to meet a person's basic physical, emotional, social or psychological needs, which is likely to result in an impairment of their well-being.

Being at risk of abuse or neglect automatically provides eligibility for care and support, even if they would otherwise fail to meet the eligibility criteria.

There is a National Independent Safeguarding Board and Local Safeguarding Boards. Much of the previous guidance is put on a statutory footing, including a duty (under sec 128) for a public body to report abuse of adults, with a similar duty in sec 130 for children.

Section 127 provides for adult protection and support orders. This enables an authorised officer of a local authority to apply for an order entitling them to speak in private to a person suspected of being at risk. There is no specific power of entry, and section 47 of the **National Assistance Act 1948** (which provided for an order to remove) has been repealed.

Code of Practice 4 provides a detailed account of the operation of an APSO. Paragraph 1.1 of the Code says:-

> "*1.1 The purposes of an APSO are:*
>
> - *to enable the authorised officer, and any other person accompanying the officer, to speak in private with a person suspected of being an adult at risk;*
> - *to enable the authorised officer to ascertain whether that person is making decisions freely; and*
> - *to enable the authorised officer properly to assess whether the person is an adult at risk and to make a decision as required by section 126(2) of the Social Services and Well-being (Wales) Act 2014 on what, if any, action should be taken.*"

An order is obtained by application to the Magistrates Court, sitting in its civil capacity. The procedure is discussed further below at paragraph 2.6 of Chapter 2 in Part D.

9. Gaining access in an emergency

The abolition of section 47 of the **National Assistance Act 1948** leaves a vacuum in terms of ways to gain access where a person is being subjected to abuse, or is at risk of neglect. The various options available for doing so are largely common to England and Wales and are dealt with in Part D. However, note the slightly different position in Wales because of the provision of adult protection and support orders under section 127 as described in the preceding paragraph.

10. Choice of Accommodation

The **Care and Support (Choice of Accommodation) (Wales) Regulations 2015 SI 2015/1840 (W.278)** permit adults in residential accommodation to choose which home they will go into, and where the cost is more than the local authority would pay, permit a "top-up" by a third party. The choice of accommodation rights in Wales now includes supported living and shared rights schemes.

The regulations (Reg 3(1)) provide that a person may choose their own accommodation provided:-

> *(a) the care and support plan for the person specifies that the person's needs can be met by the provision of care home accommodation;*
>
> *(b) the preferred accommodation is suitable to the person's needs*
>
> *(c) the preferred accommodation is available; and*
>
> *(d) where the preferred accommodation is not provided by the local authority, the provider of the accommodation agrees to provide the accommodation to the person on the local authority's terms.*

In practice this will mean that an individual generally has power over their choice of accommodation, but that this is constrained by the limitations on the local authority's budget, and the amount they are prepared to pay.

11. Human Rights Act

For the purposes of the **Human Rights Act 1998**, where care or support is arranged by a local authority, or is paid for by the local authority where the care or support is provided by a registered care provider, the care provider is deemed to be a public authority, whether the care or support is provided in a residential setting or anywhere else. Section 73 of the **Care Act 2014**, which in this respect is applicable to Wales as well, says:-

> *(1) This section applies where—*
> *... (b) in Wales, a person registered under Part 2 of the Care Standards Act 2000 provides care and support to an adult, or support to a carer, in the course of providing—*
> *(i) personal care in a place where the adult receiving the personal care is living when the personal care is provided, or*
> *(ii) residential accommodation together with nursing or personal care;*
> *...*
> *(2) The provider is to be taken for the purposes of section 6(3)(b) of the Human Rights Act 1998 (acts of public authorities) to be exercising a function of a public nature in providing the care or support, if the requirements of subsection (3) are met.*
>
> *(3) The requirements are that—*
> *(a) the care or support is arranged by an authority listed in column 1 of the Table below, or paid for (directly or indirectly, and in whole or in part) by such an authority, and*
> *(b) the authority arranges or pays for the care or support under a provision listed in the corresponding entry in column 2 of the Table.*

12. Complaints

Chapter 1 of Part 10 of the Act provides for further reform of social services complaints procedures. There are two sets of regulations, which respectively streamline the procedures for adults (the **Social Services**

Complaints Procedure (Wales) Regulations 2014 SI 2014/1794 (W.187)); and for children (**the Representations Procedure (Wales) Regulations 2014 SI 2014/1795 (W.188)**).

13. Advocacy

Chapter 3 of Part 10 to the Act governs the provision of advocacy services, and there is a comprehensive Code of Practice (number 10). Local authorities are required to arrange for the provision of an independent professional advocate when a person can only overcome the barriers to full participation in the processes described in this work with assistance from an appropriate individual, but there is otherwise no appropriate individual available. There is a range of provisions which are described in the Code, but no single provision such as that which appears in section 67 of the **Care Act 2014**.

In **R (SG) v Haringey LBC [2015] EWHC 2579 (Admin)**, the failure to appoint an independent advocate (under the provisions for appointment contained in Section 67(2) of the Care Act 2014) for a vulnerable adult who spoke no English, was illiterate, and suffered from PTSD, insomnia, depression and anxiety, rendered the assessment unlawful. As noted above, there is no directly equivalent provision for the appointment of advocates in the **Social Services and Well-Being (Wales) Act**, but the Code of Practice for Part 10 of the Act (Advocacy) makes clear the various duties to appoint an advocate, and this case is therefore likely to be of application in Wales as well.

14. Section 117 Mental Health Act 1983

Section 117 provides for after care services for patients discharged from a treatment section of the **Mental Health Act 1983** (i.e. section 3 or its criminal equivalents). Under the community care regime which predated the **Care Act 2014,** section 117 was a designated community care duty, and fell within the categories of services for which the local authority was obliged to carry out an assessment under section 47 of the

NHS & Community Care Act 1990. With the (partial) repeal of that statute, section 117 remains as a freestanding duty on the providers of care.

Because the **Social Services and Well-Being (Wales) Act 2014** does not include a duty or a power to assess for services under sec 117, the former duty to assess under sec 47 of the **National Health Service and Community Care Act 1990** has survived the general repeal of old community care statutes, and therefore remains in place as the route to sec 117 services. It follows that the **Social Services and Well-Being (Wales) Act 2014** duties regarding assessment and meeting the need do not apply to sec 117 cases.

The operative part of Sec 117 reads:-

> *117 After-care*
>
> *(1) This section applies to persons who are detained under section 3 above, or admitted to a hospital in pursuance of a hospital order made under section 37 above, or transferred to a hospital in pursuance of a hospital direction made under section 45A above or a transfer direction made under section 47 or 48 above, and then cease to be detained and (whether or not immediately after so ceasing) leave hospital.*
>
> *(2) It shall be the duty of the clinical commissioning group or local health board and of the local social services authority to provide or arrange for the provision of, in co-operation with relevant voluntary agencies, after-care services for any person to whom this section applies until such time as the clinical commissioning group or local health board and the local social services authority are satisfied that the person concerned is no longer in need of such services; but they shall not be so satisfied in the case of a community patient while he remains such a patient.*

Section 75 of the **Care Act 2014** introduces some clarifications in respect of responsibilities and ordinary residence, and also provides a definition of services. These amendments are expressed to apply to both England and Wales. The "local social services authority" is the authority for the area where the patient was resident immediately before his or her admission to hospital. Section 40 of the **Care Act 2014** (covering both countries), which covers disputes about ordinary residence, extends to a dispute as to which authority is responsible in the event of such a dispute.

Section 75 amends section 117 by introducing the following definitions. "After-care services" means:-

> "... *services which have both of the following purposes—*
> *(a) meeting a need arising from or related to the person's mental disorder; and*
> *(b) reducing the risk of a deterioration of the person's mental condition (and, accordingly, reducing the risk of the person requiring admission to a hospital again for treatment for mental disorder).*"

A new section 117A is added to the 1983 Act which provides for regulations to permit a degree of choice for a person who is being accommodated under the section, and also to confirm that those people caught by the section can top up their care and support packages.

The Care Act Guidance makes only limited provision for carers of people detained under the **Mental Health Act 1983**, and the Code of Practice in Wales does not refer to it. The best view seems to be that a carer for someone who is receiving services under section 117 is in the same position as a carer for one who is receiving services under the **Social Services and Well-Being (Wales) Act 2014**. It should also be noted that the Code of Practice for the Mental Health Act makes no reference to the position of carers of those covered by the Mental Health Act, even though it is clearly the case that they are covered.

CHAPTER FOUR: PAYING FOR CARE IN WALES

1. The Dilnot Report

Payment for social care has been a contentious issue for many years. The latest attempt to address the issue was the report of the Commission on Funding of Care and Support (the Dilnot Commission) in July 2011. The Dilnot Commission was set up in July 2010 by the coalition Government, tasked with making recommendations for changes to the funding of care and support in both England and Wales.

Prior to the coming into force of the 2014 legislation in both England and Wales, payment for residential care in both countries was governed by the **National Assistance (Assessment of Resources) Regulations 1992 SI 1992/2977**, and the system of charging for domiciliary services was contained in regulations and in guidance. In England the power to charge for domiciliary services was derived from section 17 of the **Health and Social Services and Social Security Adjudications Act 1983** (HASSASSAA); in Wales it derived from the **Social Care Charges (Wales) Measure 2010**, which amended HASSASSAA in favour of a local scheme. There was no duty to charge and, unlike residential care, there was no standard national means test. The amount charged was primarily determined by reference to what was reasonable, as outlined in Regulations and in policy guidance. The Regulations were the **Social Care Charges (Means Assessment and Determination of Charges) (Wales) Regulations 2011 SI 2011/962 (W.137)** and the Guidance was **Introducing More Consistency in Local Authorities' Charging for Non-residential Social Services,** also introduced in 2011.

Dilnot recommended that the government should set a cap on an individual's contribution towards his or her own care home care costs over their lifetime, and that the government should meet any costs in excess of that. The range suggested for the cap was between £25,000 and £50,000, although the commission itself suggested that £35,000 would be a suitable figure.

Dilnot proposed that people should in any event pay towards their living costs such as food and accommodation, but this again would be subject to a cap of between £7,000 and £10,000 a year. The upper capital limit should be raised from £23,250 to £100,000.

The report proposed that those who enter adulthood with a need for care and support should be eligible for free state support immediately, rather than being subject to a means test. Those whose need for care develops above the age of 40 should be subject to a tiered cap, starting at £10,000 for a 40 year old, £20,000 for a 50 year old, £30,000 for a 60 year old and £35,000 for a 65 year old.

The report recommended that its proposal should be implemented from 2013, and anticipated a White Paper at Easter 2012. The total expected cost of full implementation of Dilnot's proposals would have been in the region of £1.7bn a year.

2. How the Act approached Dilnot

There are two principal provisions of Dilnot which were incorporated in the new scheme in England, with a view that they would be implemented from April 2016. They have now been postponed until April 2020.

The provisions in Dilnot which have been postponed were:-

- The implementation of a lifetime cap on care costs, and
- An increase in the capital limit, which is the figure below which a person will be entitled to some contribution towards their care costs.

The Welsh Government announced its intention of looking at how a cap might operate in Wales. However, with the postponement of a care cap in England, the Welsh Government has also decided to postpone its introduction.

3. Funding of Care and Support

3.1 Legislation covering charging

The statutory provisions are contained in Part 5 of the Act. Where a person is placed in residential accommodation or is provided with domiciliary services which are funded by the local authority, the authority is entitled to make a charge if they so determine (section 59). They are also empowered by section 69 to charge for preventive services. Note that they do not have to make any charge at all. The charge may in any event not exceed the cost to the authority of its costs of meeting the need.

If they do charge, then they must follow the regulations (**Care and Support (Charging) (Wales) Regulations 2015 SI 2015/1843 (W.271)** (the "Charging Regulations") and the **Care and Support (Financial Assessment) (Wales) Regulations 2015 SI 2015/1844 (W.272)** (the "Financial Assessment Regulations"), and also the provisions of Parts 4 and 5 of the Code of Practice.

There are separate regimes for charging someone who is living in a residential setting, or at home or elsewhere in the community. However, there are a number of common features.

3.2 Needs Assessments and Financial Assessments

The normal approach to the means test is to consider only the circumstances of the individual involved, and not those of his or her spouse or partner. The Financial Assessment Regulations provide for the means test.

In the case of jointly owned income or capital, the starting presumption is that the joint owners hold it in equal shares. The local authority can assess income or capital jointly, but only where this would be more advantageous to the person concerned. See the discussion of jointly owned property in Part D.

3.3 People who lack capacity

A local authority must have policies as to how they communicate, how they carry out a financial assessment, and how they collect any charges from a person without capacity. They must consult with family members. Where possible, they should also work with someone with the legal status to make a decision; if there is no such person, then an application to the Court of Protection may be required.

3.4 Children

By Regulation 3 of the Charging Regulations, a local authority may not charge a child for care and support, or for support in the case of a young carer.

3.5 Prisoners

Where care and support is provided to a prisoner, the rules regarding a financial assessment will nevertheless be relevant. (Code of Practice 5.7)

3.6 Welfare Benefits advice

Authorities should provide appropriate welfare benefits advice to those who are to receive care and support to aid them in their understanding as to the benefits to which they may be entitled. This is expected to include a face to face discussion in the person's home, with their representative if they so require, which advises as to benefits obtainable, helps with claims, and provides follow up work. (Code of Practice 5.8)

3.7 Capital Limit

There is a standard capital limit of £24,000 (Charging Regulation 11). This applies both when determining charges for residential accommodation and for domiciliary care. A person with capital above the limit pays the whole cost of their care. A person with capital below the limit is paid for. There is no lower capital limit as in England. The rules as to deprivation continue to apply, and are discussed further in Section D.

Where a local authority places a person in residential accommodation, and that person lacks capacity, the local authority may not disclaim their liability to pay the fees on the basis that the resident has enough capital and income to be regarded as a self-funder; see **Aster Healthcare v the Estate of Mohammed Shafi [2014] EWCA Civ 1350.**

4. Contribution for those below the capital limit – means test

Certain services must be provided free of charge. These are set out at paragraph 5.12 of the Code of Practice, and include:-

- care and support provided as reablement arranged under Part 2 (General Functions) or Part 4 (Meeting Needs) of the Act, or reablement arranged as direct payments under sections 50 or 52 (Direct Payments) of the Act, to a person for up to 6 weeks to enable them to maintain or regain their ability to live independently at home.
- care and support provided to those with Creutzfeldt-Jacob Disease;
- after-care services/support provided under section 117 of the Mental Health Act 1983, discussed further above;
- the processes involved in assessing and providing services, as opposed to the services themselves. This includes the provision of information and advice;
- transport to a day service where the transport is provided as part of meeting a person's needs.
- independent professional advocacy where a local authority has arranged for the provision of this in accordance with the code of

practice on advocacy under Part 10 (Complaints, Representatives and Advocacy Services) of the Act.

In certain circumstances there is no obligation to carry out a financial assessment. (Regulation 7 Financial Assessment Regulations). These include:-

- where the local authority makes a flat rate charge (e.g. for preventative services) and it would be disproportionate to the effort involved to make a charge;
- where the person provides only limited information; in such a case, the authority may base their charge on such information as they have, if they are able to do so;
- where the person is receiving care and support for which no charge can be made.

The authority must follow the regulations set out above when carrying out the means test. Parts 4 and 5 of the Code of Practice govern financial assessments.

There is a maximum weekly charge, which is set by regulations. At the time of writing, this is £60 per week.

5. Couples and Financial assessments

The law is common to both countries and is discussed in Chapter 3 of Section D.

6. Residential accommodation

6.1 Temporary or permanent residence

Care needs to be taken to ensure that all parties are clear as to whether the occupancy is temporary or permanent, as different funding rules apply.

A person who is placed in a residential care home as part of an intermediate care package is entitled to the accommodation free of charge.

A short term resident is one whose stay is not expected to exceed eight weeks. In this case, charges are based on the calculation of charges at home, rather than as a care home resident.

6.2 Deferred Payment Agreements (DPAs)

Deferred Payment Agreements, previously covered in guidance, became statutory with the introduction of the Act. The statutory provisions are to be found in sections 34 to 36. The regulations are the **Care and Support (Deferred Payments) (Wales) Regulations 2015 SI 2015/1841 (W.269)** and the topic is covered in Annex D to Part 4 of the Code of Practice.

Local authorities **must** offer a deferred payment agreement to those persons entering or in a care home who meet certain criteria governing eligibility. The criteria are:-

(a) the person must be a person whose needs are to be met by the provision of care and support in a care home, whether this is being provided by a local authority using its duty to meet needs under section 35, or its powers to meet needs under section 36(1).

(b) the person must be one who is or will be required to pay a charge for this under section 59; and

(c) the local authority must have carried out a financial assessment under section 63.

The following conditions also apply:-

(a) the local authority must be satisfied that the person has an interest in a property which they occupy as their home, or which they used to occupy as their home;

(b) the value of this interest must not have been disregarded;

(c) the person's weekly assessed income (as calculated under the Charging Regulations) must be insufficient to meet the full care costs for their residential accommodation in a care home;

(d) the person must be in agreement with all of the terms and conditions included in the deferred payment agreement offered;

(e) the local authority must have obtained consent from any other person whom it considers has an interest over the property and which it considers may prevent it from realising the sale of the property or recovering any deferred amount;

(f) the local authority must be able to create a charge over the property which the person has an interest in and that must take priority over and rank before any other interest or charge on the property.

The authority is required to make information and advice available.

Authorities can recover administration charges for setting up and administering a DPA, and can charge interest from the first day on any amount deferred.

A deferred payment agreement can be terminated in a number of ways:

(a) where the person's capital falls below the capital limit;

(b) where the person's income becomes sufficient to meet the full cost;

(c) where the person no longer needs to live in a care home;

(d) where the person breaks the agreement;

(e) where the property becomes disregarded.

(f) at any time by the person by repaying the outstanding care costs (including any outstanding interest and administrative costs) due in full (this can happen during a person's lifetime or when the agreement is terminated through the agreement holder's death);

(g) when the property is sold and the authority is repaid; or

(h) when the person dies and the amount is repaid to the local authority from their estate.

6.3 Paying for care in residential accommodation

The basic rule is that someone with capital above the limit pays the full fee, and someone with capital below the limit pays nothing from their capital towards the cost. They may be required to contribute from their income towards the cost, but must be left with a minimum income of £26.50 per week.

PART D –
COMMON PROVISIONS
FOR BOTH COUNTRIES

CHAPTER ONE: MENTAL CAPACITY

1. Capacity

Lack of capacity is often a matter which needs to be addressed in the context of community care. The relevant legislation is the **Mental Capacity Act 2005**.

Example

David is 87. David's wife died some four years ago, since when he has lived alone in his own home. Over the past two years he has rapidly developed dementia, to the extent that he is now confused and forgetful, and often fails to recognise his family. He has become incontinent of both urine and faeces and is increasingly immobile. Consideration needs to be given to his future accommodation needs.

At present David lacks the capacity to:

- Ask for an assessment;
- Consent to an assessment if one is offered;
- Make choices as to the appropriate services which he would wish to see;
- Deal with the cost of such care;
- Manage his finances to enable him to do so.

2. The Mental Capacity Act 2005

The Mental Capacity Act 2005 introduced a structured scheme for determining whether or not a person lacks capacity to make a particular decision, and also for making decisions on behalf of a person who lacks such capacity.

2.1 Decision making under the Act

The Act aims to protect the autonomy of the individual, firstly by setting out the steps necessary to enable P (as the person concerned is referred to throughout the Act) to make a decision for him/herself if at all possible, and secondly by setting out the principles of best interests, which need to be taken into account by anyone who is charged with the task of making a decision on behalf of an incapacitated person.

The Act is supported by a comprehensive Code of Practice.

The Act begins with five general principles, which makes central the importance of autonomy:

> "*1 The principles*
>
> *(1) The following principles apply for the purposes of this Act.*
>
> *(2) A person must be assumed to have capacity unless it is established that he lacks capacity.*
>
> *(3) A person is not to be treated as unable to make a decision unless all practicable steps to help him to do so have been taken without success.*
>
> *(4) A person is not to be treated as unable to make a decision merely because he makes an unwise decision.*

> *(5) An act done, or decision made, under this Act for or on behalf of a person who lacks capacity must be done, or made, in his best interests.*
>
> *(6) Before the act is done, or the decision is made, regard must be had to whether the purpose for which it is needed can be as effectively achieved in a way that is less restrictive of the person's rights and freedom of action."*

The five principles are of general application. Capacity is issue-specific and time-specific. The starting point is the principle contained in subsection (2), which reiterates the common law presumption that a person is deemed to have capacity unless the contrary is shown. This is not merely a restatement of the common law position, and has a wider application; for example, in assessing questions of testamentary capacity, where the statutory presumption involves a change in the burden of proof.

The principles in subsections (3) and (4) emphasise the importance of assisting P to make a decision if possible and reiterate the principle that an unwise decision does not in itself mean a lack of capacity.

Subsection (5) moves on to the situation where P has been shown to lack capacity, such that matters which need to be decided for P fall to be made by another on P's behalf. Such a decision must be taken in P's best interests. Section 4 sets out the criteria to be used in determining best interests.

Finally, subsection (6) makes the additional point that, when a decision is taken on behalf of another, the least restrictive alternative should be sought.

Sections 2 and 3 go on to specify how the presence or absence of capacity is determined.

"2 People who lack capacity

(1) For the purposes of this Act, a person lacks capacity in relation to a matter if at the material time he is unable to make a decision for himself in relation to the matter because of an impairment of, or a disturbance in the functioning of, the mind or brain.

(2) It does not matter whether the impairment or disturbance is permanent or temporary.

(3) A lack of capacity cannot be established merely by reference to—

(a) a person's age or appearance, or

(b) a condition of his, or an aspect of his behaviour, which might lead others to make unjustified assumptions about his capacity.

(4) In proceedings under this Act or any other enactment, any question whether a person lacks capacity within the meaning of this Act must be decided on the balance of probabilities.

(5) No power which a person ("D") may exercise under this Act—

(a) in relation to a person who lacks capacity, or

(b) where D reasonably thinks that a person lacks capacity,

is exercisable in relation to a person under 16.

…

3 Inability to make decisions

(1) For the purposes of section 2, a person is unable to make a decision for himself if he is unable—

(a) to understand the information relevant to the decision,

(b) to retain that information,

(c) to use or weigh that information as part of the process of making the decision, or

(d) to communicate his decision (whether by talking, using sign language or any other means).

(2) A person is not to be regarded as unable to understand the information relevant to a decision if he is able to understand an explanation of it given to him in a way that is appropriate to his circumstances (using simple language, visual aids or any other means).

(3) The fact that a person is able to retain the information relevant to a decision for a short period only does not prevent him from being regarded as able to make the decision.

(4) The information relevant to a decision includes information about the reasonably foreseeable consequences of—

(a) deciding one way or another, or

(b) failing to make the decision."

Section 2(1) makes clear that capacity is both issue specific and time specific. The question is whether P had the capacity at that particular time to make that particular decision, and not whether P can be described as not having (or having) capacity in more general terms.

Subsection (3) warns against stereotyping – the fact that P is aged over 90 or has been (or indeed is) detained under the **Mental Health Act 1983**, or behaves in an odd and eccentric way, does not mean that P lacks capacity. This is often a principle that is ignored in respect of older people, or those with specific disabilities, who are assumed to lack capacity even though there is no evidence that they do.

Subsection (5) sets out the general rule that P must be at least 16 for a decision to be made on his/her behalf under the Act (although it may be made in other areas of law). The court may make a decision regarding a person under 16 if that person is likely still to lack capacity when they reach 18 (section 18(3)).

Section 3(1), developed in the remaining subsections, sets out the factors to be taken into account in determining whether P lacks capacity. P must be able to:

- Understand and retain the information necessary to make a decision, at least for a short time;
- Communicate it; and
- Foresee the consequences of the decision.

In determining whether or not P understands information, consideration must be given to the possibility that explaining the matter in a simple way will enable P to understand information which he/she could not understand if it were explained in some other way.

Example

P has a severe learning disability and is unable to speak but can respond to an issue explained to him in a very simple way. It will be possible to explain certain issues to P in such a way that he will understand (for example, 'do you want to go out this afternoon?'), but there may be difficulty in explaining to him more complex issues such as the need for medical treatment. The decision maker will need firstly to consider whether there is an easier way of explaining a more complex issue to P, and will only be able to make a decision on P's behalf if there is no way of doing so.

Chapter 2 of the Code of Practice expands on these principles. There is no sanction for non-observance of the principles, although they are likely to be relevant to one who seeks to rely on section 4(9), which provides that a person complies with the requirements of best interests if he/she has a reasonable belief that he/she is acting in P's best interests, or section 5 (acting on a reasonable belief that P lacks capacity in connection with an issue of care or treatment).

Example

Developing on the previous example, P requires an operation which is not life-threatening. D (the decision maker), having concluded that the complexities of the operation are beyond the capacity of P to understand, gives the necessary consent on P's behalf. Even though another decision maker might conclude that P had capacity to decide whether or not to undergo the medical treatment, D is able to argue a reasonable belief in P's lack of capacity, plus a reasonable belief that the decision made by D to go ahead with the operation is a decision made in P's best interests.

The statutory tests are said to reflect the common law: see, for example, **Local Authority X v MM [2007] EWHC Fam 2003** at paragraphs 73-80 (a case under the inherent jurisdiction) where Munby J (as he then was) accepts the argument that there is no real distinction between the two. The Code of Practice proceeds on the same basis: paragraph 4:33 provides:

> *"The Act's new definition of capacity is in line with the existing common law tests, and the Act does not replace them. When cases come before the court on the above issues, judges can adopt the new definition if they think it is appropriate. The Act will apply to all other cases relating to financial, healthcare or welfare decisions."*

In accepting this, Munby J points out that:

> "*... it would be worse than unfortunate if a judge of the Family Division exercising the inherent jurisdiction had to adopt an approach significantly different from the approach to be adopted by the same judge when sitting in the Court of Protection exercising the statutory jurisdiction.*"

Having said that, however, the statutory test does seem to place a stronger emphasis on enhancing the capacity of P. For example, the 'best interests' test in section 4 requires attention to be paid to P's own wishes.

2.2 Best interests

The term 'best interests' is not defined in the Act. In order to determine whether or not a prospective decision maker is acting in P's best interests, he or she needs to give consideration to the "best interests checklist" in section 4:

> "*(1) In determining for the purposes of this Act what is in a person's best interests, the person making the determination must not make it merely on the basis of –*
> *(a) the person's age or appearance, or*
> *(b) a condition of his, or an aspect of his behaviour, which might lead others to make unjustified assumptions about what might be in his best interests.*
>
> *(2) The person making the determination must consider all the relevant circumstances and, in particular, take the following steps.*
>
> *(3) He must consider –*
> *(a) whether it is likely that the person will at some time have capacity in relation to the matter in question, and*
> *(b) if it appears likely that he will, when that is likely to be.*
>
> *(4) He must, so far as reasonably practicable, permit and encourage the person to participate, or to improve his ability to participate, as*

fully as possible in any act done for him and any decision affecting him.

(5) Where the determination relates to life-sustaining treatment he must not, in considering whether the treatment is in the best interests of the person concerned, be motivated by a desire to bring about his death.

(6) He must consider, so far as reasonably ascertainable –
(a) the person's past and present wishes and feelings (and, in particular, any relevant written statement made by him when he had capacity),
(b) the beliefs and values that would be likely to influence his decision if he had capacity, and
(c) the other factors that he would be likely to consider if he were able to do so.

(7) He must take into account, if it is practicable and appropriate to consult them, the views of –
(a) anyone named by the person as someone to be consulted on the matter in question or on matters of that kind,
(b) anyone engaged in caring for the person or interested in his welfare,
(c) any donee of a lasting power of attorney granted by the person, and
(d) any deputy appointed for the person by the court, as to what would be in the person's best interests and, in particular, as to the matters mentioned in subsection (6)."

Subsection (1) again warns against stereotyping. The remainder of the section lists the matters to be taken into account in making a decision, which overall leads to two basic questions. What would P have wanted? What do others think P might have wanted?

Example

In the drawing up of a statutory will (where the Court is asked to make a will for someone who lacks the capacity to do so), two people are considered. P1 has learning disabilities and has not been able to communicate since birth. Because of that condition, there will be no pre-existing will, and those drafting a statutory will are likely to need to assess whether it would be appropriate to vary the rules on intestacy, so as to include provision for some person who might otherwise not benefit, or so as to tip the balance of the distribution of the estate in favour of those people to whom P1 is likely to feel indebted. This decision must take P1's best interests into account.

On the other hand, P2 has lost capacity relatively late in life, but has a history of making and amending wills as lifetime events cause decisions already made to be reconsidered. In such a case, there is already a history available of P2's wishes and feelings, values and beliefs, and a decision is likely closely to reflect P2's previous approach to the issue of disposing of his/her estate.

The best interests duties also apply to the exercise of any powers under a Lasting Power of Attorney (LPA) (see below), or by anyone else who makes a decision for someone whom they believe to lack capacity (section 4(8)). In other words, the best interests test is of universal application. In addition, deputies appointed by the Court of Protection, attorneys under LPAs and professionals are bound to have regard to the Code of Practice (section 42(4)). This extends to any court or tribunal which is hearing proceedings. It will, for example, be relevant when the Court of Protection is asked to remove a deputy or to revoke an LPA under section 16(8) or 22(3)(b) when satisfied that that person has behaved, is behaving or proposes to behave in a way that is not in the best interests of P.

The decision as to best interests is also affected, as noted previously, by section 4(9) –

> *"In the case of an act done, or a decision made, by a person other than the court, there is sufficient compliance with this section if (having complied with the requirements of subsections (1) to (7)) he reasonably believes that what he does or decides is in the best interests of the person concerned."*

Not all these factors will be relevant in every case. They should, however, all be considered, if only in order to be discounted. No one factor takes priority.

The obligation to involve P in the decision should be noted. If P is likely to regain capacity to make the decision for him/herself at some time in the future, it should be considered whether the decision can be delayed to enable P to do so. However, this may need to be balanced with the fact that a delay may itself not be in P's best interests. Chapter 3 of the Code of Practice suggests a range of steps which can help and encourage P to participate in decision making.

The checklist does not mean that the approach is to try to determine what P would have wanted, and to follow that regardless.

3. The Code of Practice

Section 42 of the Act directed the Lord Chancellor to produce one or more Codes of Practice to guide those working with the Act. The Code was issued on 23 April 2007. There has been a supplementary code issued to cover the Deprivation of Liberty Safeguards (DoLS) which were introduced by the **Mental Health Act 2007**.

Section 42(4) of the Act lists those who have a duty to have regard to the Code, namely:

- The donee of a Lasting Power of Attorney (LPA);
- A deputy appointed by the Court;

- A person carrying out research in reliance on any provision under the Act;
- An Independent Mental Capacity Advocate (**Mental Capacity Act 2005**); and
- Anyone acting in a professional capacity or for remuneration.

Donees of Enduring Powers of Attorney (EPAs) (the forerunners of LPAs) are not included. There is no penalty for failure to abide by the Code, but a Court may take breaches into account.

Non-professional and informal decision makers (such as carers) are not bound by the Code unless they fall into one of the other categories. A donee of an LPA is bound by the Code and this should be drawn to their attention when a Power is being drawn up.

4. Decision making and the inherent jurisdiction

What is the status of the inherent jurisdiction of the High Court since the coming into force of the Act? In **Westminster City Council v IC, KC, NNC [2008] EWCA Civ 198**, the Court of Appeal confirmed that the inherent jurisdiction continues to exist alongside the Act. This was also considered in the case of **DL v A Local Authority and others [2012] EWCA Civ 253.** This will be of use where the person seeking protection may be defined as a 'vulnerable adult' (as was the case in DL) but has mental capacity and therefore cannot call on the Act for protection. In both cases cited, the Court of Appeal rejected the argument that the Act was the only refuge for a vulnerable person.

The inherent jurisdiction may therefore provide a solution where P does not in fact lack capacity but his/her will is overborne, perhaps because of P's own limited ability to cope which does not amount to incapacity (see, for example, the 'forced marriage' cases such as **A Local Authority v MA, NA, SA [2005] EWHC 2942 (Admin)**).

5. Lasting Powers of Attorney

Lasting powers of attorney (LPAs) are intended to enable a person (P) to appoint an attorney who is able to act on his or her behalf after P has lost capacity. This is contrary to the normal rule that authority under a power of attorney depends on the capacity of the donor. LPAs cover both financial matters and decisions as to health and care.

Sections 9 – 14, and Schedule 1, of the **Mental Capacity Act 2005** provide for the creation and administration of LPAs. There are two types of LPA: finance, and health and care. In both cases P may nominate one or more people to act as attorney, and if he or she so chooses may also nominate one or more people to act as a replacement attorney in the event of the death or incapacitation of one or more of the original attorneys. P must also provide one or more "certificate providers" – a friend, or a professional – who is able to certify that P understands what he or she is doing by making the LPA, and that s/he is not under any undue pressure to persuade him or her to make it.

In the case of a finance LPA, P is offered the opportunity to state in the LPA whether it is to come into effect immediately, or only when P no longer has capacity. A health LPA only comes into effect once P has lost capacity.

The LPA must be registered with the Office of the Public Guardian, and a fee of £85 paid. This can be done at any time, though it is often more suitable to register as soon as the LPA is executed, given the possible delays in registration at the OPG, and the fact that, if P has lost capacity when the power comes to be registered, and there are errors, it is too late to correct them. By way of encouraging immediate registration, the standard LPA forms now include not only the power of attorney itself, but an application for registration.

A health and care attorney is usually entitled to be consulted regarding the care of the person for whom s/he is attorney.

6. Advance Decisions

6.1 The Mental Capacity Act 2005 Provisions

Section 24 of the Mental Capacity Act 2005 defines an advance decision as follows:-

> *"(1)"Advance Decision" means a decision made by a person ("P"), after he has reached 18 and when he has capacity to do so, that if–*
>
> *(a) At a later time and in such circumstances as he may specify, a specified treatment is proposed to be carried out or continued by a person providing healthcare for him, and*
>
> *(b) At that time he lacks capacity to consent to the carrying out or continuation of the treatment*
>
> *- the specified treatment is not to be carried out or continued.*

It is not necessary for any specific language to be used, in particular the technical titles of any specific medical treatment. The decision need not be in writing unless it is intended to give directions regarding life sustaining treatment, when it must be signed and witnessed (section 25(5)). The advance decision may be withdrawn at any time when P has capacity, and such withdrawal need not be in writing. An alteration of an advance decision need not be in writing either (but a failure to render a decision into writing may cause evidential problems).

Section 25 covers the validity and applicability of advance decisions. An advance decision is not valid if P

- has withdrawn the decision at a time when he or she had capacity;
- has conferred authority on attorneys under an LPA executed subsequent to the AD (see below);
- has done anything clearly inconsistent with the AD

An AD is not applicable if P has the capacity to give or refuse consent at the time. Nor is an AD applicable in the following situations:-

- the treatment is not the treatment specified in the AD
- any circumstances specified in the AD are absent
- there are reasonable grounds for believing that circumstances exist which P did not anticipate and which would have affected his or her decision

As noted, an AD in respect of the withholding of life sustaining treatment must be in writing. It must be signed by P, or by another person in P's presence and at P's direction, and must be signed by a witness. A letter containing the necessary instructions is not sufficient unless the signature is witnessed **(An NHS Trust v D [2012] EWHC 885 (COP))**

The effect of a valid and applicable AD is that, at the time when the question of providing the treatment concerned arises, P's decision made while he or she had capacity is treated as if it were made at the time when the treatment is being proposed, even though P now lacks capacity to make that decision. It is legally binding.

Under section 26, the person treating incurs no liability for doing so unless he or she is satisfied that there is a valid and applicable AD, and nevertheless treats P in the face of it. The person treating does not incur liability for withholding or withdrawing treatment if satisfied that he or she is doing so on a basis of a valid and applicable AD.

The court has power to make a declaration as to whether an AD exists, is valid, or is applicable to a treatment.

Nothing in an apparent AD stops a person providing life sustaining treatment, or doing any act necessary to prevent a serious deterioration in P's condition, while a decision as to the validity or otherwise of the AD is sought from the court (section 26(5)).

6.2 LPAs and Advance Decisions

By section 25 of the **Mental Capacity Act 2005**:-

> *(2) An advance decision is not valid if P—*
> *(a) has withdrawn the decision at a time when he had capacity to do so,*
> *(b) has, under a lasting power of attorney created after the advance decision was made, conferred authority on the donee (or, if more than one, any of them) to give or refuse consent to the treatment to which the advance decision relates, or*
> *(c) has done anything else clearly inconsistent with the advance decision remaining his fixed decision.*
> ...
> *(7) The existence of any lasting power of attorney other than one of a description mentioned in subsection (2)(b) does not prevent the advance decision from being regarded as valid and applicable.*

The issue usually (but not necessarily) concerns life sustaining treatment. By an AD, P gives directions which are legally binding provided P has capacity at the time they are given; but a health and care LPA may delegate the power to discontinue life sustaining treatment to a third party (the attorney). If this can be regarded as a subsequent decision, it will render the AD invalid. An example of the problems which might arise is found in **N and anor v E and ors [2014] EWCOP 27** where the LPA post-dated the AD (and therefore superseded it) but the attorneys under the LPA itself subsequently disclaimed their attorneyships, thereby leaving neither the LPA nor the AD in place to give effect to P's wishes. The court resolved the issue by making a declaration in accordance with section 26(4) of the **Mental Capacity Act 2005** to give effect to P's wishes as set out in the original AD.

6.3 The liability of health care professionals

As well as protection under section 26 (referred to above), if there is reasonable belief that an AD exists and no search is made to confirm this, liability may arise. Failing to follow a valid and applicable Advance Decision may result in both civil and criminal sanctions.

Health care practitioners are protected from liability under **Mental Capacity Act 2005** sec 5, providing they act in P's best interests where there is no valid and applicable AD, or they are following a valid and applicable AD.

The Mental Capacity Act, sec 5 says

> *(2) D does not incur any liability in relation to the act that he would not have incurred if P –*
>
> *(a) had had capacity to consent in relation to the matter, and*
>
> *(b) had consented to D's doing the act.*
>
> *(3) Nothing in this section excludes a person's civil liability for loss or damage, or his criminal liability, resulting from his negligence in doing the act.*

CHAPTER TWO: GAINING ACCESS IN AN EMERGENCY

2.1 Introduction

This section considers the problems firstly of a person who is being subjected by those caring for him or her to some level of abuse or neglect, and secondly of a person who is unable to care for him or herself, where that person is either living somewhere where they are being prevented from leaving, or living in inappropriate conditions which they are unwilling to leave, or to remedy the conditions rendering the premises inappropriate. How is access to be gained to that person in order to carry out appropriate safeguarding tasks?

The abolition of section 47 of the **National Assistance Act 1948** (see above) leaves a vacuum in terms of ways to gain access where a person is being subjected to abuse, or is at risk of neglect. This section considers some of the powers available to gain access.

2.2 Under the Mental Capacity Act 2005

The Court of Protection has the power, under section 16(2) of the Act, to make an order affecting the welfare of a person who lacks capacity. A penal notice may be attached to such an order. The Court may also appoint a deputy, and can make interim orders and directions under section 48 where P is believed to lack capacity and it is in their best interests to make an order without delay. The Court will be slow to make an order against a third party, but will do so if necessary – see for example **Re SA; FA v Mr A [2010] EWCA Civ 1128.**

2.3 Under the inherent jurisdiction

If a person lacks capacity, the correct method of proceeding is by way of the Mental Capacity Act. If they do not, however, the High Court can be asked to exercise its inherent jurisdiction. See for example **LB of Redbridge v G [2014] EWHC 485 (COP)**. Again the order may be made against a third party; see **A Local Authority v DL [2010] EWHC 2675, [2012] EWCA Civ 253** (above).

If capacity is in doubt, and it is decided to proceed in the first instance by way of the Court of Protection, it will be convenient if the Court of Protection judge is also a High Court judge who can, as an alternative, exercise the inherent jurisdiction.

2.4 Under the Mental Health Act 1983

Under Section 115 of the **Mental Health Act 1983**, an approved mental health professional (AMHP) may at all reasonable times enter and inspect any premises (other than a hospital) in which a mentally disordered person is living, if there is reasonable cause to believe that the person is not receiving proper care.

The section does not allow for forced entry, but obstructing an AMHP could be an offence under sec 129 of the **Mental Health Act 1983**.

In a more serious case, where there is suspected neglect or abuse of a person with a mental disorder, a magistrate has power to issue a warrant under sec 135 **Mental Health Act 1983** authorising a police officer to enter and remove the person to a place of safety. Detention under this section lasts for up to 72 hours, giving time for a **Mental Health Act 1983** assessment to be commenced.

In **R (Sessay) v South London and Maudsley NHS Foundation Trust [2011] EWHC 2617 (QB)**, police entered the claimant's private accommodation, unaccompanied and without a warrant under section 135. They purported to be acting in her best interests under sections 5 and 6 of the **Mental Capacity Act 2005**. She was taken to hospital and, after a 13-hour delay in the section 136 suite, she was detained under section 2 of the **Mental Health Act 1983**. It was held that Sections 5 and 6 **Mental Capacity Act 2005** do not confer on police officers authority to remove persons to hospital or other places of safety for the purposes set out in sections 135 and 136. The **Mental Health Act 1983** provides a complete statutory code for compulsory admission to hospital for non-compliant incapacitated patients, so the common law doctrine of necessity does not apply during the period in which a patient is being assessed for detention under the Act. If there is urgent necessity to detain then the **Mental Health Act 1983** section 4 emergency procedure should be followed

2.5 Under police powers

There are various powers available to the police both under the **Police and Criminal Evidence Act 1984** (PACE) and at common law. Under section 17(1)(b) of **PACE** the police have power to enter and arrest where an indictable offence has been committed. Under section 17(1)(e) they have power to enter and search premises without a warrant in order to "save life and limb" – this means that the police must be concerned about serious bodily injury (see **Baker v CPS [2009] EWHC 299**).

Under section 24 of **PACE**, the police may arrest a person who has committed, is committing, or is about to commit an offence. The grounds are to protect a vulnerable person likely to be harmed or at risk of being harmed if the person in question is not arrested, and other arrangements for the prevention or harm cannot be made in order to protect the vulnerable person.

Finally, there is a common law power of entry to deal with a breach of the peace. This will normally only apply in an emergency. See for example **Blench v DPP [2004] EWHC 2717.**

2.6 Adult Protection and Control Orders (Wales Only)

As noted above, in Wales there is a power to seek an order for access from the Magistrates Court. Section 127 of the **Social Services and Well-Being (Wales) Act 2014** allows for an order to be made to enable an authorised officer to speak privately to a person suspected of being an adult at risk, in order to determine whether he or she can take decisions freely, with a view then to establishing what, if any, action should be taken.

An authorised officer is one authorised by the local authority, subject to the regulations as to who can be appointed (the **Adult Protection and Support Orders (Authorised Officer) (Wales) Regulations 2015 SI No 2015/1465 (W.159)**).

Once the order is in force, the authorised officer, together with a police constable if necessary, and any other person specified in the order, may enter the premises where the suspected adult at risk is living, for the purposes of the order, and if necessary with the use of reasonable force by the police officer.

An adult protection and support order can only be granted if the court is satisfied that –

(a) the authorised officer has reasonable cause to suspect that a person is an adult at risk,

(b) it is necessary for the authorised officer to gain access to the person in order properly to assess whether the person is an adult at risk and to make a decision as to what, if any, action should be taken,

(c) making an order is necessary in order to fulfil the purposes set out in subsection (2), and

(d) exercising the power of entry conferred by the order will not result in the person being at greater risk of abuse or neglect.
Statutory guidance has been issued. See
http://gov.wales/docs/phhs/publications/160404part7guidevol1en.pdf

CHAPTER THREE: WHAT SERVICES ARE REQUIRED TO MEET THE NEED

1. Ways of meeting the need

In both jurisdictions it is clear that, where the criteria for eligibility are met, the local authority is under a duty to meet the needs for care and support, or for support, as appropriate. This section considers how those needs are to be met, how far the authority is bound to comply with the wishes of the individual, and the possibility of challenges where it is not considered that the local authority has acted appropriately to meet the needs identified.

It is generally the case that the courts will largely expect the authority to make decisions within their own parameters, and the court is unlikely to interfere if due process is followed. This is largely confirmed by the Supreme Court case of *R* (*McDonald*) *v* **Royal Borough of** *Kensington* & *Chelsea* [**2011**] **UKSC 33**, later considered by the European Court of Human Rights in **McDonald v. the United Kingdom ECHR 141 (2014)**. Although the judges in the Supreme Court made clear that dignity was a factor to be considered, the majority preferred to leave it to the authority to ensure that dignity was respected.

2. Dignity

Other cases, both before and after **McDonald**, have considered the issue of dignity, and have found breaches of Article 8 of the European Convention, or even of Article 3. In **R (Clarke) v LB Sutton** [**2015**] **EWHC 1081 (Admin)**, care was provided for Mr Clarke in supported accommodation by the London Borough of Enfield. He became ordinarily resident in the London Borough of Sutton, which initially decided to continue to provide the same service, but which later revised that decision on the basis of cost. The Court held (inter alia) that Article 8 was engaged, and Mr Clarke succeeded in his claim. The burden on the claimant will be a heavy one, following the test laid down in **R (Ireneschild) v LB Lambeth** [**2007**] **EWCA Civ 234**, requiring procedural irregularity or unreasonableness verging on absurdity. Nevertheless the Court held that the claimant had met the test in the particular case and quashed the decision of Sutton.

There have been several cases where the failure to meet the claimant's right to dignity has led to breaches of the claimant's convention rights, for example **R (A, B, X and Y) v East Sussex CC** [2003] **EWHC 167; R (Burke) v General Medical Council and others** [2004] **EWHC 1879; and R (Bernard) v Enfield LBC** [2002] **EWHC 2282.** In the first case, Munby J (as he then was) considered both the European Convention and also the Charter of Fundamental Rights of the European Union, citing among other provisions Articles 1 and 3 of the Charter:-

> "*1 Human dignity is inviolable. It must be respected and protected. 3(1) Everyone has the right to respect for his or her physical and mental integrity.*"

He went on to consider dignity and its importance in particular in the interpretation of Article 3 of the European Convention, drawing attention among other authorities to the case of **Price v United Kingdom (2001) 34 EHRR 1285** and quoting with approval the judgement of the court at paragraph 1294:

> "*There is no evidence in this case of any positive intention to humiliate or debase the applicant. However, the Court considers that to detain a severely disabled person in conditions where she is dangerously cold, risks developing sores because her bed is too hard or unreachable, and is unable to go to the toilet or keep clean without the greatest of difficulty, constitutes degrading treatment contrary to Article 3.*"

Neither case appears to have been cited to the Supreme Court in **McDonald (Bernard** was cited in the judgement of Lord Brown). The case may provide some assistance with mounting an argument based on dignity.

3. The effect of the new legislation

The other issue of relevance is the construction of the two new statutes, in particular taking into account the well-being duty, and also the emphasis on outcomes as opposed to services. The English Act provides, in Section 1:-

> *(2) "Well-being", in relation to an individual, means that individual's well-being so far as relating to any of the following—*
> *(a) personal dignity (including treatment of the individual with respect);*
> *(b) physical and mental health and emotional well-being;*
> *(c) protection from abuse and neglect;*
> *(d) control by the individual over day-to-day life (including over care and support, or support, provided to the individual and the way in which it is provided);*
> *(e) participation in work, education, training or recreation;*
> *(f) social and economic well-being;*
> *(g) domestic, family and personal relationships;*
> *(h) suitability of living accommodation;*
> *(i) the individual's contribution to society.*

And the Welsh Act provides, in section 2:-

> *(2) "Well-being", in relation to a person, means well-being in relation to any of the following—*
> *(a) physical and mental health and emotional well-being;*
> *(b) protection from abuse and neglect;*
> *(c) education, training and recreation;*
> *(d) domestic, family and personal relationships;*
> *(e) contribution made to society;*
> *(f) securing rights and entitlements;*
> *(g) social and economic well-being;*
> *(h) suitability of living accommodation.*

It is interesting to note that 'dignity' appears in the English, but not the Welsh, definition.

In **Re MN (Adult) [2015] EWCA Civ 411**, the CA held that the Court of Protection had no power to require a social services authority to provide different services, but only to consider whether the services provided were in P's best interests. Any challenge to the sufficiency of services offered had to be by way of judicial review. The decision was confirmed (sub nom. **N v ACCG and others** [2017] **UKSC 22**) by the Supreme Court on 22 March 2017. It is apparent that any challenge must be brought as a judicial review.

Early cases on the new law have started to give an indication of how "well-being" may be interpreted. **R (Davey) v Oxfordshire County Council** [2017] **EWHC 354**, was a challenge to a local authority decision to cut the provision of services to a man with severe quadri-plegic cerebral palsy. His personal budget was cut from £1,651 to £950 per week. Part of his care package had been funded by the Independent Living Fund prior to its closure, and then by the local authority in its entirety.

Morris J held that the well-being duty in section 1 of the **Care Act** was

> "*... a duty, when taking decisions, to have regard to each person's particular individual circumstances and not to make generalised assumptions based on characteristics such as age, physical condition etc.*"

It was important to distinguish between needs and wishes, and the duty of the authority was to meet the former and not the latter. As part of the process of determining services, the care user must be involved in the making of their care plan, and the local authority must take all reasonable steps to reach agreement with the care user. However, there was no outright duty to reach an agreement if this was not possible after taking reasonable steps

On the other hand, in **R (JF) v Merton LBC** [2017] **EWHC 1519 (Admin)** the Court quashed an assessment as unlawful, among other things because of the failure of the local authority properly to apply the well-being principle. JF, a young man aged 24 with complex needs, was the subject of an assessment by Merton, and a decision as a result of that assessment that he should be moved. Anne Whyte QC, sitting as a deputy High Court Judge, held (at para 47):

> "*In my judgment the Needs Assessment must specify what JF's needs are and it must do so on a rational basis. If the Assessment failed to assess the impact of JF's needs for care and support upon the factors of wellbeing listed in section 1(2) of the Act, then it is an unlawful assessment. Likewise, if it failed to assess the outcomes that JF's wishes to achieve in day-to-day life, and whether, and if so to what extent, the provision of care and support could contribute to the achievement of those outcomes, it is unlawful. If it fails to have regard to the matters specified in Regulation 3(2) as set out in paragraph 30 above, it is unlawful. If the author failed to have regard to the wishes and preferences of the individual (expressed here to a degree by the Guardians, his parents), then it is unlawful. If it is neither appropriate nor proportionate then it is unlawful.*"

The matters specified in Regulation 3(2) to which the Judge refers are (a) the wishes and preferences of the individual to whom it relates; (b) the outcome the individual seeks from the assessment; and (c) the severity and overall extent of the individual's needs.

The court additionally found, at para 61, that no reasonable local authority would terminate the placement of someone with JF's complex needs without having conducted a lawful assessment of those needs and without having lawfully decided that suitable alternative accommodation was available that would enable them to meet his needs.

Although the approach to well-being differs slightly between the two Acts, both find their origin in the same report of the Law Commission, and both adopt the principle of well-being, although there are differences between the two Acts in the way in which that principle is set out. The case would therefore appear to be applicable to Wales as well as to England.

Ombudsman cases may be of assistance. In **Complaint against Hammersmith and Fulham LBC (LGO Complaint number 15 011 661, 21 July 2016)**, Ms J, who has a sight impairment, sought direct payments because her care agency did not help her to organise her clothes so that she could dress correctly, to organise her fridge so that she did not miss dates on food packaging, and to scan documents. The local authority reviewed her care plan and found that she had no unmet needs. A local charity could assist with computer issues, and the **Care Act 2014** did not require her to wear matching or clean clothes, or eat fresh food rather than long life products. The LGO found it was maladministration (i) to respond to her initial request with a review of her care package; (ii) not to assess how she would fare if the charity was unable to help her; not to recognise the importance to her dignity of wearing clean and matching clothes; (iv) not to recognise the importance of eating fresh food. The **Eligibility Regulations** include outcomes of 'managing and maintaining nutrition' (which is clearly wider than eating to stay alive) and 'being appropriately clothed' (which is also wider than being able to wear dirty and mismatched clothes), so there appears to be a legal error as well as maladministration.

Separately from the powers under the **Care Act 2014**, the local authority's 'general power of competence' under the **Localism Act 2011** may be of use. In **R (GS) v Camden LBC [2016] EWHC 1762 (Admin)**, it was noted that, although the claimant had no right to accommodation under the **Care Act 2014**, section 1 of the **Localism Act 2011** empowered Camden to provide the claimant with accommodation, and on the facts they were required to do so to avoid a breach of her rights under the European Convention on Human Rights (see Chapter 7 of this Part, below) resulting from her homelessness and lack of sufficient means to support herself.

CHAPTER FOUR: MATTERS AFFECTING FINANCIAL ASSESSMENTS

1. Couples and Financial assessments

Unlike the benefits system, neither the **Care Act 2014** nor the **Social Services and Well-Being (Wales) Act 2014**, in carrying out financial assessments, requires the aggregation of the needs and resources of a couple. The consequence is that each person should be assessed according to their individual means. This may prove difficult if the financial resources of a couple are inextricably linked, and care should be taken to separate the two where one partner goes into a care home, in order that the capital of one partner should not be used to meet the care home costs of the other.

Where there is joint beneficial ownership of capital other than real property, the charging regulations deal with the question of its division. The English and Welsh regulations are worded identically. Regulation 24 of the **Care and Support (Charging and Assessment of Resources) Regulations 2014 SI 2014/2672** ("English Charging Regulations") says:-

> *(1) Where the adult and one or more other persons are beneficially entitled in possession to any capital asset except an interest in land*
>
> *—*
>
> *(a) unless paragraph (2) applies, each person is to be treated as if each of them were entitled in possession to an equal share of the whole beneficial interest; and*
> *(b) that asset is to be treated as if it were actual capital.*
>
> *(2) This paragraph applies where the local authority is satisfied that the adult is beneficially entitled in possession to a share which is less than or, as the case may be, more than an equal share of the whole beneficial estate.*
>
> *(3) Where paragraph (2) applies the adult's share of the whole beneficial interest will be the actual share (as determined by the local authority) and is to be treated as if it were actual capital.*

The Welsh equivalent is Regulation 24 of the **Care and Support (Financial Assessment) (Wales) Regulations 2015 SI 2015/1844 (W.272)** ("Welsh Charging Regulations").

In either case there is clearly scope for arguing that jointly owned property other than land (for example money in a joint account) is in fact owned in unequal shares.

In a case where the resident is receiving an occupational pension, a personal pension, or payment from a retirement annuity contract, and he or she has a spouse or civil partner who is not living in the same care home, 50% of that payment should be disregarded provided the resident passes 50% on to the spouse. (English Charging Regulations, Schedule 1, Para 16; Welsh Charging Regulations, Schedule 1, Para 15.)

2. Jointly Owned Property

Curiously, neither set of charging regulations deals with the issue of jointly owned real property. It will therefore be likely that an assessor will turn to the law which was developed previously, much of which is to be found in benefits law. As noted above, both the English and the Welsh charging regulations provide that, with the exception of land, where there is a jointly owned asset the authority must treat it as owned in equal shares unless they are satisfied that the shares are in fact not equal; and it seems likely that the same procedure will be followed in the case of land. In most cases this situation will arise where one of a couple ("the resident") has entered residential care, but the other has not.

Where the resident legally owns any property but has no beneficial interest in it, he or she is a trustee and the value of the property should not be taken into account.

Where the resident is a joint beneficial owner of property, then the interest to be valued as the resident's capital is the value of that interest, not the property itself. If the property is owned as joint tenants, then the starting point may well be to treat each joint tenant as having an equal share. However, where there is a tenancy in common, the starting point will be the value of the share of the tenant in common (**Hourigan v Secretary of State for Work and Pensions [2002] EWCA Civ 1890**). The ultimate issue is the question whether the resident is able to assign the beneficial interest to someone else, and to the availability of a market for such an interest. If that is the case, the effect may possibly be that the value of the share is nil.

It would normally be the case that one of co-owners could force a sale; but where the property was purchased jointly as a home for both, it is unlikely that a sale will be ordered. See **Chief Adjudication Officer v Palfrey [1995] 11 LS Gaz R 39**, CA. However, where the acquisition was for other reasons this may not apply. See **Wilkinson v Chief Adjudication Officer [2000] EWCA Civ 88**. Mrs Wilkinson's mother died in August 1995 and left her freehold house to Mrs Wilkinson and her brother. The Will provided that they were to take it in equal shares, and they could do as they wished with it. The house was worth £59,000, and had a secured charge on it of almost £14,000. The house was empty from August 1995 when Mrs Wilkinson's mother died, until 1997. At that point, Mrs Wilkinson's brother returned from Australia to live in it.

Mrs Wilkinson was a single parent with 3 dependent children, and was receiving income support. She did not disclose her inheritance until April 1997. On 26 June 1997, her half share in the house was valued at £13,846. She argued that the amount should have been valued as nil. The Court of Appeal took the view that **Palfrey** was not a relevant authority, and a sale could be compelled.

3. Sale of assets to pay care home fees

In **Re RGS No 2 (CoP 11831647)**, RGS was in a residential care home. His son RBS removed him on the grounds that he was not being adequately cared for and was being deprived of his liberty. Complex proceedings followed and eventually by consent RGS was returned to the care home on a best interests basis. The Court also appointed Essex County Council to act as his deputy as there was evidence that RBS had acted inappropriately with regard to his father's money. The Council decided to sell a number of his paintings and artworks to fund his care, including an original Pissarro, and applied to the Court for permission to sell them. The District Judge, having concluded that RBS lacked the capacity to conduct proceedings, appointed a litigation friend to act on his behalf. The Court made the necessary order, formally by consent, although in fact against vigorous opposition from RBS.

The judge noted,

> "*In an ideal world, the Pissarro painting would be passed by father to son or daughter, and be a treasured keepsake. If his father still had capacity to appreciate the painting, I am sure that he would prefer that. However, the regulations require that the cost of RGS's care is paid for from his own assets and it is no longer possible to keep the painting. The position would be the same if he still had capacity to make that decision for himself.*"

It might be observed that there is a possible tension between the duties of the local authority in acting as RGS's deputy and their duty to ensure payment of his care home fees. As the judge noted, it is irrelevant to the operation of the charging regulations that RGS had no capacity to deal with the management of his property; it was in his best interests that he reside in a care home, and it was necessary for him to pay the costs of doing so (section 7 of the **Mental Capacity Act 2005** regarding payment for necessaries may also be of relevance), although he had no way of doing so other than by the sale of his assets.

4. Care home fees and continuing health care

In **Harrison v South Tyneside Council HM Land Registry Adjudicator Decision Ref/2012/886**, Mr Jackson had dementia and lacked mental capacity. He was placed by the council in residential accommodation until he died. His administrator pursued several arguments in respect of the fees. He suggested that the costs ought to have been borne as part of continuing health care (see this Part, Chapter 8), and alternatively that Mr Jackson should have been sectioned under the **Mental Health Act 1983** because he lacked the capacity to consent to be admitted to the care home and did not require it because he had his own home. In rejecting the arguments, the Deputy Adjudicator held:

> "*4. In my judgment, Mr Jackson did avail himself of the accommodation despite his lack of capacity. It was accommodation which he required to receive the necessary care and attention not otherwise available to him and the fact that he lacked capacity to understand that does not mean that he did not avail himself of it within the meaning of the* [**National Assistance Act 1948**]. *I would add that if that were not the case, then the provision of the accommodation would in the circumstances have been a necessary either at common law or under section 7 of the* ***Mental Capacity Act 2005****, and he would have been obliged to pay a reasonable price for it, which would have been recoverable from his estate (****Wychavon District Council v EM*** **[2012] UKUT 12 (AAC))."**

The fact that he had his own home was irrelevant if he needed care and attention which was not available to him there (para 6). Thus, the local authority was able to declare a charge on the property pursuant to what was then section 22 of the **Health and Social Services and Social Security Adjudications Act 1983**. If this power were absent (and it may be noted that it was removed by the 2014 legislation), the local authority would be entirely unprotected in the absence of an LPA or a Court order.

CHAPTER FIVE: DEPRIVATION OF CAPITAL

1. The Capital Rule

Where a person has capital above the limit, the local authority may not pay for any services provided, and the entire cost falls on the person themselves. There is therefore an incentive to minimise capital in order to qualify for a contribution, and this may take the form of giving capital away. This is known as deprivation of capital.

It most commonly affects the payment of care home fees. Where a person receives care in their own home, the rules on deprivation are unlikely to be applied, since in most cases it is the disposal of the home which prompts the application of the rules; but the same rules apply to issues of deprivation of other assets which would otherwise be taken into account in carrying out the means test.

Where a care home resident reduces his or her capital to a figure below the upper limit, however, the local authority may well look at the circumstances in which capital was reduced, and take action if appropriate. If the reduction was for the purpose of becoming entitled to funding, this is deprivation of capital, and the authority can respond by way of the "notional capital rule" in order to prevent the individual relying on that deprivation to gain funding.

Rules on deprivation of capital are effectively the same in both jurisdictions, although the power to deal with it is legislated differently. In England the rule is to be found in reg 22(1) of the **Care and Support (Charging and Assessment of Resources) Regulations 2014 SI 2014/2672** which provides:-

> *22.—(1) The adult is to be treated as possessing capital of which the adult has deprived themselves for the purpose of decreasing the amount that they may be liable to pay towards the cost of meeting their needs for care and support, or their needs for support …*
>
> *(4) Where the adult is treated as possessing capital under paragraph (1) or (2), the provisions of this Part apply for the purposes*

of calculating its amount as if it were actual capital the adult does possess.

The relevant Guidance is at paragraph 8.27 et seq. and at Annex E. Regulation 22 of the **Care and Support (Financial Assessment) (Wales) Regulations 2015 SI 2015/1844 (W.272)** provides in similar terms:-

> *22.—(1) A is to be treated as possessing capital of which A has deprived themselves for the purpose of decreasing the amount that they may be liable to pay, reimburse or contribute towards the cost of the care and support to meet their needs ...*

The relevant part of the Code of Practice is Parts 4 and 5, paragraph 8, and Annex F.

2. Giving the home away

This considers the situation where a client seeks to save care home fees by for example transferring a substantial asset (such as their house) to a third party (commonly a child or children). How should a client who proposes to do so be advised?

There are a number of issues to be considered before such a step is taken. Among the first is the advisability of such a step, and its possible effects, given that the donor will initially have no security at all if they give their house to their children. This part of the discussion should also include consideration of what will happen if the children fall out with one another or with the parent, or if a child becomes bankrupt or divorces and a third party makes a claim on the property.

The second is its effectiveness. With the coming into force of both the **Care Act 2014** and the **Social Services and Well-Being (Wales) Act 2014**, the previous limitation on taking action against the donees directly (that this must be done within six months of the gift) has been removed. Action can therefore always follow against the donees. Even if this is not the case, the local authority has various options open to it to challenge the disposition.

Consideration should first be given to the question of whether it is necessary at all. This includes the following issues:-

• **What are the chances of going into care?**

This is commonly overstated. It is often asserted that there is a significant chance, of up to 50%, of an older person needing to go into residential or nursing care. Although the chances of doing so do increase with age, an attempt should be made properly to assess the chances of an individual, with their personal circumstances and health needs, going into care at some future date.

• **Does the house belong to the donor, free from incumbrance, at all?**

Consider the possibility that the house, or part of it, in fact is held in trust for a third party. This may apply, for example, where a person has bought a former council house (or, indeed, any other property) with money provided by another – say a child. It is possible that all or part of the house is therefore held on a resulting trust for that third party, even if there is no formal document saying so. See for example **Nottingham City Council v Berresford [2011] EWLandRA 2010_0577** (HM Land Registry Adjudicator), where funding for the purchase was provided by the children and was supported by a declaration of trust which was executed some 12 years later, and also **Brighton CC v Audus [2009] EWHC 340 (Ch)**, where there was a carefully drawn up agreement under which the provider of the funds was the beneficial owner of the property even though it was in the names of the older couple to whom he provided funding. In both cases the result was a finding of others having an interest in the house.

In assessing proportions for ownership purposes, remember in the case of a council house to include consideration of the discount made on a purchase price to a former council house tenant.

Consider also the possibility of other incumbrances, such as a claim based on proprietary estoppel.

- **Is it worth it?**

It may need to be pointed out to the client that the test is not whether they own a house, but whether they have capital. It achieves nothing to give away a house but to retain other capital (e.g. in stocks and shares) which exceeds the capital limit, and most people will be unwilling to give away their entire fortune – even assuming this would work!

- **Is the house exempt as capital?**

While the house is occupied by the individual, its value will be irrelevant for the purpose of paying for care. Even after that person has left, the house may fall to be disregarded in certain circumstances.

It must be disregarded if occupied by a spouse, civil partner, or cohabitee; by a relative who is aged over 60, or is incapacitated; or by anyone under 18. This is a mandatory disregard. The local authority also has a discretion to disregard it if it is occupied by anyone at all (e.g. a younger child who has given up their own house to care for their parent). In all such cases, the occupier is required to occupy the property as their 'only or main' home; see **Walford v Worcestershire CC [2015] EWCA Civ 22**. The judge at first instance had held that a "home" was a place to which a person had a degree of attachment both physical and emotional, and it followed that a person could be deemed to 'occupy' the premises even if they did not live there all the time, or even for the majority of the time. This was unchallenged in the appeal, and maybe taken to represent the law. The Court of Appeal, by a majority, nevertheless allowed the authority's appeal; they held that the determination of whether the disregard exists should take place on the date that the resident went into residential care. Any determination of "home" therefore required both a qualitative and a quantitative assessment. The Court of Appeal's decision in **Walford** is reflected in the statutory guidance and the Code of Practice on the subject of disregards.

3. Dealing with deprivation of capital

There are several possibilities open to the local authority to challenge a deprivation, the main ones being to apply the deprivation of capital rules under section 72 of the Act, or alternatively to proceed by taking action under the **Insolvency Act 1986** sec 423.

Note that under the Act the authority has no power to set aside a transaction, but may seek to recover its expenditure from any gift of capital which is caught by the rules.

Although the application of the rule may leave uncertain the funding position for care, the authority's duties to the individual do not disappear, and they may remain under a duty to provide accommodation to that person – although where the person is already in accommodation, this may not necessarily be the same accommodation.

4. The Consequences of Deprivation

Section 70 of the **Care Act 2014** and section 72 of the **Social Services and Well-Being (Wales) Act 2014** are couched in almost identical terms. The Welsh legislation states:-

> ***Transfer of assets to avoid charge***
>
> *(1) This section applies in a case where the needs of a person ("P") have been or are being met by a local authority under sections 35 to 42 or section 45 and where—*
> *(a) a person ("the transferor") (who may be P but need not be so) has transferred an asset to another person (a "transferee"),*
> *(b) the transfer was undertaken with the intention of avoiding charges for having P's needs met, and*
> *(c) either the consideration for the transfer was less than the value of the asset or there was no consideration for the transfer.*

> *(2) The transferee is liable to pay to the local authority an amount equal to the difference between—*
> *(a) the amount the authority would have charged the transferor were it not for the transfer of the asset, and*
> *(b) the amount it did in fact charge the transferor.*
>
> *(3) But the transferee is not liable to pay to the authority an amount which exceeds the benefit accruing to the transferee from the transfer.*
>
> *(4) Where an asset has been transferred to more than one transferee, the liability of each transferee is in proportion to the benefit accruing to that transferee from the transfer.*

The authority therefore has scope for proceeding against any transferee of the property.

As regards the previous owner, however, there is also the option of applying the notional capital rule as set out in Regulation 22 of the **Care and Support (Charging and Assessment of Resources) Regulations 2014 SI 2014/2672**, and in Regulation 22 of the **Care and Support (Financial Assessment) (Wales) Regulations 2015 SI 2015/1844 (W.272)**, as noted above. In such a case the notional capital rule applies, the person is treated as if they still owned the capital in question, and if this increases their capital above the upper limit, they are disqualified for local authority funding.

It is likely that case law decided under the previous law is still of full effect. In reaching a decision, therefore, the purpose and timing of the deprivation need to be considered. The leading case in England and Wales is **R (Personal Representatives of Beeson) v Dorset CC and the Secretary of State for Health** [2001] **EWHC Admin 986, (2002) 5 CCLR 5)**, affirmed [2002] **EWCA Civ 1812**. In that case, a 90-year old man in poor health made a gift of his house to his son. He suffered a stroke and was admitted to hospital; he was discharged to his own home, but some 2 years later, was placed permanently in residential care. He died at the age of 95 at the time of the first instance hearing.

The court found evidence to support the view that his purpose was to provide a home for his son in the event of the son becoming homeless following a divorce, and that he had no intention of going into residential care. The court held that it is this subjective approach which is appropriate. In making the disposition, what was in the resident's mind?

The case distinguished the Scottish case of **Yule (Yule v South Lanarkshire Council 2000 SLT 1849)**, which took a harder line. In that case the Inner House of the Scottish Court of Session held that the local authority was entitled to infer intention, and that indeed they could do so from age alone. Mrs Yule was aged 78 and in good health. The Court considered that it was unnecessary for the applicant to know of the capital limit (benefits law refers to knowledge of 'a' capital limit, and says that it is unnecessary for the individual to know the actual amount), and that the authority can draw a reasonable inference from the circumstances that it must have been a purpose of the transaction to avoid having to pay charges. No specific finding is required as to the exact state of knowledge or intention of the resident.

In **Beeson** there was evidence from the resident's family about his state of mind at the relevant time. This included the fact that he had knowledge of the capital limit. Richards J in **Beeson** said,

> "*Although the court [in **Yule**] held that it is not necessary for the claimant to know of 'the' capital limit and that no specific finding is required as to the exact state of knowledge or intention of the applicant, I do not see how an applicant could be found to have the relevant purpose unless he was aware of the possibility that he might be provided with accommodation and that he might be liable to pay for it.*"

In other words, the appropriate test is a subjective one. **Yule** arguably permits an objective test, but this is incompatible with the **Beeson** approach.

Annex F to Part 4 of the Welsh Code makes clear the requirement for the authority to examine the subjective intention and purpose at the time of the transfer, and furthermore that the intention to avoid the charge must be a significant purpose of any transfer. Paragraph 1(3) advises:-

> "*Where a person accrues a debt the local authority should take all reasonable steps to ascertain the reason this has occurred and must not assume that the person is deliberately not meeting a charge imposed for care and support, or for support if a carer. A local authority must seek to establish the reason for a debt accruing and only where it is clear that it is as a result of a person's deliberate non-payment should they consider debt recovery.*"

And Annex E to the English guidance states:-

> *11) There may be many reasons for a person depriving themselves of an asset. A local authority should therefore consider the following before deciding whether deprivation for the purpose of avoiding care and support charges has occurred:*
> *(a) whether avoiding the care and support charge was a significant motivation in the timing of the disposal of the asset; at the point the capital was disposed of could the person have a reasonable expectation of the need for care and support?*
> *(b) did the person have a reasonable expectation of needing to contribute to the cost of their eligible care needs?*

5. Deprivation and section 423

An alternative approach for the local authority is via **section 423** of the **Insolvency Act 1986.** The court may set aside a transaction which is entered into at an undervalue. This refers to a transaction made at any time if (a) it consists of a gift or a transfer for no consideration, or (b) it is in consideration of marriage, or (c) it is for a consideration the value of which, in money or money's worth, is significantly less than the value, in money or money's worth, of the consideration provided by the transferor. The transaction must have taken place for the purpose –

(a) of putting assets beyond the reach of the person who is making, or may at some time make, a claim against the transferor, or

(b) of otherwise prejudicing the interests of such person in relation to the claim which he is making or may make.

A decision by an individual to gift their house to their children, in order to avoid care home fees, would clearly be caught by this section if the necessary intention was present. See, for example, **Derbyshire County Council and another v Akrill [2005] EWCA Civ 308**, upholding a first instance decision.

Note the requirement to have carried out the transaction *for the purpose* of putting assets beyond reach, so attention needs to be paid to the resident's intention, i.e. it is a subjective test. Cases such as **Yule** and **Beeson** may therefore be relevant.

Where the section applies, the court may make such an order as it thinks fit for –

(a) restoring the position to what it would have been if the transaction had not been entered into, and

(b) protecting the interests of persons who are victims of the transaction.

There is no time limit on section 423 and it is not necessary for the resident to be made bankrupt. Proof of dishonesty is not required, "merely proof of avoidance of creditors whether they be existing or future creditors" (**Midland Bank v Wyatt [1995] 1 FLR 697**).

Where a local authority is faced with an apparent deprivation, the issue is likely to be firstly whether they can expect to succeed on the basis of the subjective test. If they can, then they can simply refuse the application for funding and leave the resident to challenge this.

The problem which then remains, however, concerns the continuing duty of the authority. Under section 21 of the **National Assistance Act 1948**, the authority's duty to accommodate is not made subject to sorting out who is to pay for it (though if they are not being paid, the authority is likely to consider moving the resident to cheaper accommodation. It may be noted that they can do this provided the risks are properly assessed: see **R (Watts) v Wolverhampton City Council [2009] EWCA Civ 1168**). Where the resident qualifies, the authority has a duty to provide the accommodation first and (in effect) to consider payment for it later.

> "*The assessment of need and decisions as to whether they call for the provision of any of the community care services comes first. The assessment of needs and the requirement to pay what the person can afford, comes later. Notional capital can be taken into account at the stage when charges are being made for the services. But it must be left out of account at the earlier stage when decisions are being taken to provide these services.*"

(Robertson v Fife Borough Council [2002] **UKHL 35, per Lord Hope of Craighead)**

Herein lies the attraction of proceedings under section 423, although this is to some extent offset by the removal of the time limit on the authority proceeding against the donee of a gift. Both proceedings rely on the subjective intention of the claimant. However, even successful use of the deprivation rules will not remove the duty to continue to provide accommodation – and in the case of (for example) a house which has been given to children, there is then probably no asset available which can help to meet the accommodation charges provided under that duty. If, on the other hand, that gift can be set aside using section 423, then compensation can be secured for the authority without compromising their duty to accommodate.

CHAPTER SIX: ORDINARY RESIDENCE

Ordinary residence is covered in the **Care Act 2014**, sections 39 to 41; and in the **Social Services and Well-Being (Wales) Act 2014,** sections 194 and 195. It is relevant because it determines the duties that a local authority may owe towards a service user or a carer.

The previous case law (in particular **R v Barnet LBC ex parte Shah [1983] 1 All ER 226**) remains relevant, in particular the judgement of Lord Scarman:

> *"... unless ... it can be shown that the statutory framework or the legal context in which the words are used requires a different meaning I unhesitatingly subscribe to the view that ordinarily resident refers to a man's abode in a particular place or country which he has adopted voluntarily and for settled purposes as part of the regular order of his life for the time being, whether of short or of long duration."*

The case of **R (Cornwall) v Sec of State for Health** [2015] **UKSC 46** must now also be considered. Guidance issued by the Department of Health as a result of the case has now been incorporated into the Statutory Guidance.

For a person who lacks capacity to make decisions about their accommodation, and for children transitioning into adult social care services, **Cornwall** holds that a person's lack of mental capacity may mean that they are not able voluntarily to adopt a particular place of residence. The Supreme Court held that a child who had been placed in foster care in local authority A, which had been arranged by local authority B under the **Children Act 1989**, continued to be ordinarily resident in local authority B when he reached 18 years of age. The principle laid down by the Supreme Court (para 54) is that

> *"... an authority should not be able to export its responsibility for providing the necessary accommodation by exporting the person who is in need of it"*

In the later case of **Re B [2016] UKSC 4**, the Supreme Court held, in the context of the new conceptions of habitual residence within the family sphere (which itself draws particularly on recent cases at the European Court) that it will only be in very limited cases where a child will have no habitual residence. Judges in the Court of Protection (see for example **Re SW [2014] EWCOP 43**) have made it clear that the rules for determining the habitual residence of those with impaired capacity should be the same as those for children.

There are significant 'deeming' rules concerning ordinary residence in the legislation. The first concerns adults in NHS accommodation, who are deemed both by section 39(5) of the **Care Act 2014**, and by section 194(4) of the **Social Services and Well-Being (Wales) Act 2014**, to be ordinarily resident in the area where they were immediately before their admission.

The second concerns those for whom the local authority arranges accommodation in the area of another local authority. The rule is that the person is deemed ordinarily resident in the area where they were ordinarily resident immediately before the placement began or, if they were not ordinarily resident anywhere, in the area where they were present. This previously covered only those for whom the arranged accommodation was in a registered care home. Section 39(1) of the **Care Act 2014** now provides that the rule covers those living in specified accommodation, and the **Care and Support (Ordinary Residence) (Specified Accommodation) Regulations 2014, SI No 2014/2828**, provide that "specified accommodation" includes care homes, shared lives scheme accommodation and supported living accommodation. The same statutory provision appears in section 194(1) of the **Social Services and Well-Being (Wales) Act 2014**, by reference to accommodation specified in regulations, but the only accommodation specified in the **Care and Support (Ordinary Residence) (Specified Accommodation) (Wales) Regulations 2015, SI No 2015/1499 (W.171)**, is care home accommodation.

In addition, under section 39(4), someone who is provided with accommodation under section 117 of the **Mental Health Act 1983** is deemed to be ordinarily resident in the area of the local authority which arranged for the accommodation to be provided. This provision is expressed by the **Care Act 2014** to apply to both England and Wales, and the provision is repeated in section 194 (4A) of the **Social Services and Well-Being (Wales) Act 2014.**

The ordinary residence provisions are liable to result in local authority disputes, and section 40 of the **Care Act 2014**, applicable to both countries, sets up a mechanism whereby such disputes can be resolved.

CHAPTER SEVEN: PEOPLE FROM ABROAD

Section 21 of the **Care Act 2014**, and section 46 of the **Social Services and Well-Being (Wales) Act 2014**, both pick up on the provisions in previous legislation which limit the access to accommodation of a "person from abroad" under section 21 of the **National Assistance Act 1948**. This restriction was imposed following the interpretation of the provision in section 21 that the local authority's duty to accommodate arose where a person was in need of care and attention which was not otherwise available to them "by reason of age, illness, disability **or other circumstances**" (emphasis added). Arguments had been successfully mounted (in **R v Hammersmith LBC ex parte M, 1 CCLR 85**) that an asylum seeker may have needs which were due to "other circumstances". The local authority's duty to provide accommodation was thereby activated.

As a result legislation, originally in the **Asylum and Immigration Act 1996**, and later in the **Immigration and Asylum Act 1999**, provided that, in the case of a person subject to immigration control under section 115 of the **Immigration and Asylum Act 1999**, such rights should not arise where the need for care and support had arisen as a result of destitution; the argument being that the National Asylum Support Service was responsible for meeting any such needs.

The provision concerning the meeting of the needs of asylum seekers, which now rests with local authorities, consists of a power, under section 95 of the **Immigration and Asylum Act 1999**, to provide services to asylum seekers, or their dependants, who are 'destitute'. Destitute means having no adequate accommodation, or having no way of meeting essential living needs. In order to preserve the policy that the provision of such services is a matter for asylum support and not for community care, sections 21 of the **Care Act 2014** and 46 of the **Social Services and Well-Being (Wales) Act 2014**, as appropriate, apply. Those covered are those within the ambit of Section 115 of the **Immigration and Asylum Act 1999**, which applies to non-EEA nationals who

- have no leave to enter or remain but require it, or
- have a no recourse to public funds condition, or
- have leave which is subject to a maintenance undertaking.

Subsequent case law, however (**R. v Wandsworth LBC Ex p. O; R. v Leicester City Council Ex p. Bhikha** [2000] **1 W.L.R. 2539**) establishes that a need for assistance under what was formerly s.21 of the 1948 Act (provision of accommodation) does not arise "solely" from destitution where that need is to any material extent made more acute by some circumstance other than the mere lack of accommodation or funds, such as age, illness or disability. This test is known as the "destitute plus test".

Section 21 of the **Care Act 2014**, and section 46 of the **Social Services and Well-Being (Wales) Act 2014**, maintain the original policy that support in the case of destitution is a matter for asylum support, and support in the case of "destitution plus" is a matter for community care. Further, the two sections extend the bar to cover all provision to meet needs for care and support, and not just the provision of accommodation.

A person from abroad is, on the face of it, just as entitled as anyone else to an assessment and to the provision of services. What potentially disentitles them is the barring procedure in sections 21 and 46. The order is important; a person subject to immigration control has the same rights under the Act as anyone else, unless the barring procedure impinges.

The barring procedure now therefore says that a local authority may not meet the needs of a person subject to immigration control who needs care and support where needs for care and support have arisen solely as a result of destitution or its effects. It does not prevent the making of provision in cases of "destitution plus", and it does not affect any duty or power to provide support to a carer.

The barred services include services under Part 1 **Care Act 2014** and under the **Social Services and Well-Being (Wales) Act 2014**. It also includes services under Section 1 of the **Localism Act 2011**. Barred people include those who have refugee status abroad, EEA nationals, and certain failed asylum seekers (Para 1 Sch 3 **Nationality Immigration and Asylum Act 2002**). Local authorities are generally prohibited from providing services to those barred.

There is one significant exemption to the rule, which follows from the case of **R (Limbuela) v Secretary of State for the Home Department [2005] UKHL 66**. The prohibition does not apply where the refusal of services would amount to a breach of his or her human rights, in particular Article 3 of the European Convention. This would be the case where the person, with

> "*no alternative sources of support, unable to support himself, is, by the deliberate action of the state, denied shelter, food or the most basic necessities of life.*"

Although she did not say that this should be the test, Baroness Hale, in **Limbuela**, suggested (at para 78) that cashlessness + rooflessness = inhuman and degrading treatment:

> "*It might be possible to endure rooflessness for some time without degradation if one had enough to eat and somewhere to wash oneself and one's clothing. It might be possible to endure cashlessness for some time if one had a roof and basic meals and hygiene facilities provided. But to have to endure the indefinite prospect of both, unless one is in a place where it is both possible and legal to live off the land, is in today's society both inhuman and degrading.*"

The issue of state provision for persons from abroad, interlinked as it is with asylum and immigration law, is a complex area, and resort should be had to the specialist texts in the area to ensure that the correct approach is followed.

CHAPTER EIGHT: THE INTERFACE BETWEEN HEALTH AND SOCIAL CARE

1. The Alternatives

Where a person is to receive care, it is necessary to determine how the cost is to be met, and hence to determine what sort of care it is. There are three alternatives:-

- NHS continuing health care; the whole of the person's care is funded by the NHS and is free of charge to the person concerned.
- Funded nursing care; that part of the care of a person in a nursing home which is considered to be nursing care is funded by the NHS, and the rest of their care falls to the individual or their local authority.
- Ordinary "social care" which is not the responsibility of the NHS at all. It is paid for by the individual, with support from the local authority.

2. Health Care and Social Care

Whereas care which is provided by the NHS for a medical need is free at the point of use, care for other matters (usually described as 'social care') provided by or through local authorities is subject to charge under either the **Care Act 2014** or the **Social Services and Well-Being (Wales) Act 2014.** Because of the need to define who pays for care is important, the distinction between health and social care remains contentious, and this distinction has been subject to a number of challenges.

In **R v North and East Devon Health Authority ex parte Coughlan [2000] 2 WLR 622,** following a catastrophic accident in which she was knocked from her bike, Pamela Coughlan was firstly accommodated in a hospital, and then subsequently in a long stay facility provided by the NHS. When that facility was closed, she was relocated into independent accommodation with services provided in part by the local authority. The dispute centred on eligibility criteria agreed between the health authority and the local authority as to what services constituted health care (free at the point of use) and what constituted social care (provided by the local authority and therefore chargeable). The Court of Appeal held that social services could only fund low level nursing care. The eligibility criteria could not impose on the local authority a responsibility which goes beyond their powers; and the criteria as established and applied in the particular case were therefore unlawful.

Fresh guidance was issued by the Department of Health (**HSC 2001/015: LAC (2001) 18**). The system of the Registered Nursing Care Contributions (see below) was introduced, which enabled the provision by the NHS of a contribution towards the nursing (i.e. health) needs of those living in a nursing home, but this was no more than sticking plaster (although it is still in place). Reliance on the guidance could give rise to a gap between local authority and health entitlements, as noted by the judge in **R (T, D and B) v Haringey LBC [2005] EWHC 2235 (Admin)**, and this gap was addressed directly in the case of **R (Grogan) v Bexley NHS Care Trust [2006] EWHC 44 (Admin)**, which heavily criticised the guidance mentioned above.

As a consequence the **National Framework for Continuing Health Care** was issued in England in June 2007. The current framework was revised in November 2012. The Welsh equivalent was issued in 2010, with revised guidance in 2014. NHS Continuing Health Care is largely outside the scope of this work, but is included because of its interface with other provisions. Although there are differences between the two regimes, it is convenient to consider them together.

3. NHS Continuing Health Care

Continuing health care is the term used when a person's needs are considered to be health needs payable by the NHS. It has been defined as

> *"A package of care arranged and funded solely by the health service for a person aged 18 or over to meet physical or mental health needs which have arisen as a result of illness."*

(Direction 1 of the **NHS Continuing Healthcare (Responsibilities) Directions 2007**)

Clinical Commissioning Groups in England, and Local Health Boards in Wales, are responsible for promoting awareness of the policy, and for ensuring that it is properly implemented. Care can be provided in any setting, including a patient's own home or a care home. The CCG or the LHB, as appropriate, is responsible for deciding eligibility. If the person is eligible, the CCG or LHB arranges funds for care. The question of where the person shall live is then secondary.

For England, the Guidance, the three assessment tools which enable decisions on entitlement to continuing health care to be met, and the Directions can be found on the Gov.UK website. For Wales, the documentation is on the gov.wales website. The references are:-
https://www.gov.uk/government/uploads/system/uploads/attachment_data/file/213137/National Framework-for-NHS-CHC-NHS-FNC-Nov-2012.pdf http://gov.wales/docs/dhss/publications/140630frameworken.pdf http://gov.wales/docs/dhss/publications/140630supporttoolen.pdf

The issue of whether someone is entitled to claim continuing health care is likely to be of major importance to many people. It is a matter which needs to be considered, in appropriate cases, by a deputy or an attorney. Where there was an unrecognised entitlement to continuing health care, it may be possible for an individual to reclaim expenditure on care costs. Where the person has died, their personal representatives may need to consider a claim. It may be noted that the Department of Health has placed limitations on the time for which such a claim can go back.

3.1 Eligibility and assessment

Eligibility is a matter for the Clinical Commissioning Group or Local Health Board, as appropriate.

Consent should be sought before the assessment takes place. The patient can choose a family member or other person to advocate on their behalf. (English Guidance paras 33-35; Welsh Guidance paras 2.54 – 2.56)

If the patient lacks capacity to consent, it should be determined whether any other person (such as an Attorney) has the responsibility for giving consent under the provisions of the **Mental Capacity Act 2005**, or whether the patient has made an Advance Decision. If not, then action must be taken in the patient's best interests. If the patient lacks capacity, and there is no appropriate relative or carer to be consulted, then consideration should be given to the appointment of an Independent Mental Capacity Advocate (sections 35 to 41 **Mental Capacity Act 2005**), in cases where serious medical treatment or change of accommodation is proposed.

3.2 Procedure

The full assessment is carried out using the matrix below. In England, pending a full assessment, there will usually be a shorter form of assessment to ascertain the likelihood of the patient qualifying for CHC. There is no such intermediate step in Wales. The matrix is the same in both countries.

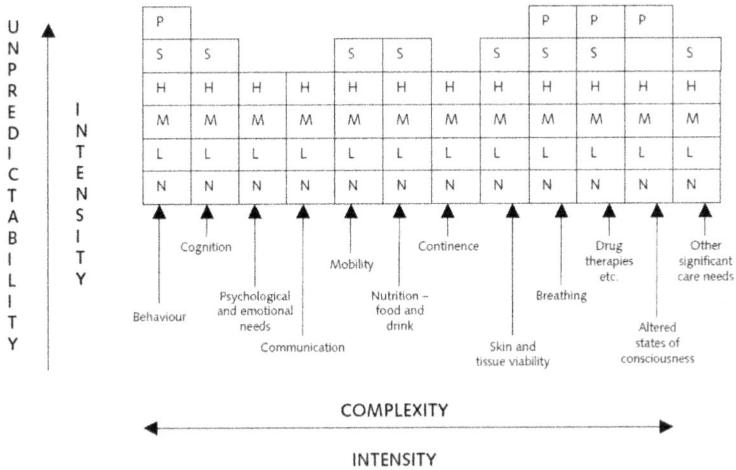

Source: National Framework for NHS Continuing Healthcare and NHS-funded Nursing Care: November 2012 (revised), p29

3.3 What is covered

The aim of the CHC programme is that the NHS should be responsible for all the costs of a person's care, as they would if s/he were in hospital, and this is so regardless of where the person lives. This will include care related housing costs. However, the Court of Appeal has reminded funders that the duty to cover all costs does not extend to cover payment for ordinary housing costs. In **R (Whapples) v Birmingham CCG [2015] EWCA Civ 435**, the court held that

> *"... read as a whole, the National Framework does not, in circumstances where a patient is receiving continuing NHS healthcare in his own home, generally contemplate that the NHS will be responsible for defraying the costs of that accommodation." (at para 32, per Burnett LJ)*

The Court referred with approval to the Practice Guidance contained within Part 2 of the English 2012 Framework.

3.4 The effect on benefits

The most likely of any possible consequent effects is that which will affect the benefits for disability: attendance allowance, personal independence payments, and disability living allowance. The general rule is that these benefits cease after 28 days in a hospital or care home, provided the individual is not responsible for their own funding in either situation. Where the person remains at home, the receipt of NHS CHC does not affect their benefits at all. Where the person is in a nursing home, they will generally be treated as an NHS inpatient for benefit purposes, and the 28 day rule will apply. It will not, however, apply in other circumstances. See **Secretary of State for Work and Pensions v Slavin [2011] EWCA Civ 1515**, where the Court of Appeal dealt with the issue of a claimant living in a privately run care home whose funding is being met by the NHS. The claimant had a number of health problems including autistic traits and challenging behaviour. His fees in the care home were paid by the health authority. The care home was staffed by appropriately qualified people, but they had no staff with any medical or nursing qualifications. Before moving into the care home in 2007, the claimant had been living with his parents and was receiving the higher rate of the mobility component and the highest rate of the care component of DLA.

When he moved into the care home, the Department for Work and Pensions decided that neither component was payable because he was 'being maintained free of charge while undergoing medical or other treatment as an inpatient... in a hospital or similar institution...' for the purposes of regulation 8 (care component) and regulation 12a (mobility component) of the **Social Security (Disability Living Allowance) Regulations 1991**'. His appeal was dismissed by a tribunal but allowed in the Upper Tribunal by Judge Turnbull (**CDLA/3638/2008**). The Secretary of State then appealed to the Court of Appeal.

The Court of Appeal dismissed the Secretary of State's appeal. Richards LJ held that, although the claimant's healthcare needs qualified him for an NHS funded residential placement at a care home,

> "*... it does not seem to me to be a natural use of language to describe him as 'undergoing medical or other treatment as an inpatient... in a hospital or similar institution', in the terms of regs 8 and 12A. The authorities show that the condition is to be given a somewhat wider meaning than might appear at first sight, but in my view they do not lead to a construction of the condition which would bring the respondent's situation within it.*" (paragraph 52)

The judge also says that the care received by the claimant from staff in the care home does not amount to nursing.

> "*It is true that they look after residents who, in the case of the respondent at least, suffer from a disability of the mind amounting to 'illness', but it does not follow that the care that they provide is nursing care; and in my view it can fairly be described as domestic care (or 'personal' care, within the meaning of section 3(1) of the Care Standards Act 2000) rather than nursing care.*" (paragraph 55).

It may be commented that the failure to provide a useful definition of nursing care has bedevilled the law and practice which is designed to govern the provision of any sort of care.

4. Funded Nursing Care

Local authorities are prevented by **section 49 of the Health and Social Care Act 2001** from providing nursing care by a registered nurse. Where a resident of a nursing home has a care need, therefore, it will be necessary to determine how the care is to be provided.

If the need is a 'primary need' for nursing care, the full costs of providing all that resident's care (nursing and non-nursing) are borne by the NHS under the continuing health care provisions. Where the resident requires some nursing care, but nursing is not his or her primary need, the NHS will pay only part of the care costs. This contribution is known as 'Funded Nursing Care' ("FNC") (formerly Registered Nursing Care Contributions). FNC is a contribution which is laid down in regulations. The rate is £155.05 per week from 1 April 2017, with the higher rate available to certain longstanding recipients of care being set at £213.32.

In such a case, dependent upon means, the resident in question and/or the relevant local authority is responsible for paying for the remainder of the care costs.

Recently the Court of Appeal has considered the interface between these two positions. The case is a Welsh one and is concerned with Welsh Local Health Boards, but the case is of more general application. In **R (Forge Care Homes) v Cardiff and Vale University Health Board [2016] EWCA Civ 26**, the Court of Appeal overturned a decision by Hickinbottom J (**[2015] EWHC 601**) which had held that the NHS was responsible for paying for social care which is delivered by a registered nurse. The seven Health Boards affected duly appealed and their appeal was successful.

In practice, the Court of Appeal judgment means that:

- It is for the NHS to decide what type of care does and does not need to be provided by a registered nurse, and only fund the former;
- Local authorities and self-funders may need to pick up any shortfall where a nurse provides services that the NHS does not deem to be nursing care.

The Department of Health (which intervened in the Court of Appeal) is currently in the process of reconsidering the manner in which it calculates the FNC rate. The Court of Appeal's judgment is bound to affect the shape of that reconsideration. Both NHS bodies and local authorities may wish to have a say in this ongoing process.

The case was appealed to the Supreme Court which considered it on 26th April 2017 (case number 2016/0054), but judgement had not been delivered by the time of publication. The issue for determination by the Court is:-

> "*Whether the NHS (through Local Health Boards) is required to fund registered nurses in care homes only when they are providing nursing care or also when they are providing social care to certain residents.*"

MORE BOOKS BY LAW BRIEF PUBLISHING

A selection of our other titles available now:

'The Law of Driverless Cars: An Introduction' by Alex Glassbrook
'A Practical Guide to Costs in Personal Injury Cases' by Matthew Hoe
'A Practical Guide to Alternative Dispute Resolution in Personal Injury Claims – Getting the Most Out of ADR Post-Jackson' by Peter Causton, Nichola Evans, James Arrowsmith
'A Practical Guide to Personal Injuries in Sport' by Adam Walker & Patricia Leonard
'A Practical Guide to Marketing for Lawyers' by Catherine Bailey & Jennet Ingram
'The No Nonsense Solicitors' Practice: A Guide To Running Your Firm' by Bettina Brueggemann
'Baby Steps: A Guide to Maternity Leave and Maternity Pay' by Leah Waller
'The Queen's Counsel Lawyer's Omnibus: 20 Years of Cartoons from the Times 1993-2013' by Alex Steuart Williams

These books and more are available to order online direct from the publisher at www.lawbriefpublishing.com, where you can also read free sample chapters. For any queries, contact us on 0844 587 2383 or mail@lawbriefpublishing.com.

Our books are also usually in stock at www.amazon.co.uk with free next day delivery for Prime members, and at good legal bookshops such as Hammicks and Wildy & Sons.

We are regularly launching new books in our series of practical day-to-day practitioners' guides. Visit our website and join our free newsletter to be kept informed and to receive special offers, free chapters, etc.

You can also follow us on Twitter at www.twitter.com/lawbriefpub.

Lightning Source UK Ltd.
Milton Keynes UK
UKOW06f1941281117
313525UK00004B/111/P